*RHYME & * REASON:

THE POETRY OF LEADERSHIP

To Roisin, for inspiration — to & fror....! — with love Sam x

Sam Chittenden

Rhyme & Reason:

The Poetry of Leadership

Different Development

Published in the United Kingdom by:

Different Development
55 Roundhill Crescent
Brighton, BN2 3FQ
www.differentdevelopment.com

Printed in the United Kingdom

First Printing, 2014

ISBN 978-0-9930880-0-1

DEDICATION

For Simon, my late-found love, whose faith makes everything possible

For my children Joseph, Hannah, Jake & Liberty, my greatest teachers

&

For my clients, whose trust & courage are constant sources of inspiration

Love & gratitude, always

◻   ◻   ◻

Contents

1	Introduction: Leadership As Poetry	1
2	What is Leadership?	9
3	What is Poetry?	17
4	Poetry as a Metaphor for Leadership	25
5	A Place For Poetry	35
6	The Poetic Leader	45
7	The Language of Leadership	57
8	The Leader's Voice	71
9	A Vocation: Letting Your Life Speak	89
10	Sounding it Out: Rhyme & Resonance	99
11	Leading with Rhythm: A Cadence of Work	113
12	Shape Making: Structure, Form & Space	129
13	Telling the Truth	147
14	Showing & Telling	159
15	Story & Narrative	171
16	Finding Meaning; Making Sense	183
17	Thinking & Learning	193
18	Sustaining Creativity	207
19	Heart To Heart: Making Connections	215
	Bibliography	229
	Acknowledgements	233
	References	241

A knotting of words
net hauling silver to light
making connections

Beth Somerford

1

INTRODUCTION: LEADERSHIP AS POETRY

I will not follow where the path may lead,
but I will go where there is no path, and I will leave a trail.

From *Wind-Wafted Wild Flowers*, Muriel Strode

Introduction

In this book I explore the concept of *leadership* through the metaphor, language and structure of *poetry,* and consider how the choices made in any leadership role have their parallels in that creative world. I aim to offer a way of seeing leadership - leadership as poetry - that can serve as a guide for leaders and leadership development practitioners.

Genesis

I spent over 25 years of my career working in the British National Health Service, most of that time as a senior leader and board member. Like many of my colleagues, I seemed to fall into a management career, and found myself seeking whatever information might help me get my head around the conundrum of how to lead. I read books and looked for role models and mentors.

Whilst there was lots of information and advice out there, little of it spoke to me. Most of the management training that was on offer seemed formulaic and directive. I was searching for a way to approach leadership that would push the right buttons for me, not just tick the boxes. There were glimpses of ideas and images that made sense - such as one particularly encouraging boss, a conference workshop by *Olivier Mythodrama,* and the narrative approach used by a coach I worked with - but I wasn't able to weave them together into a coherent whole. Such glimpses were at odds with much of my day-to-day experience.

One realisation was that a huge amount of my individual skill and passion was not being used at work. As I started to work as a coach and mentor, I heard similar frustrations from coachee after coachee.

Another seminal moment was taking part in the personal development workshop *The Mastery of Self Expression*. At the workshop, which was created by Dan Fauci at the Actors' Institute in New York, I discovered my voice and a new, integrated, sense of myself. I also found a joy of performing and of reading my poetry in public. I knew that I needed a way to blend these aspects of who I am in my work, and set myself the dual goals of bringing more creativity to my leadership role, and of finding ways of leading through creativity; that was the genesis of this book.

I realised that I needed to find not only a place in the world, but a way of seeing that place - and my role in it - that enabled me to truly plant my feet. As I started to think about when I was most creative at work, and what worked about my leadership style, I kept finding resonance and connections. The idea of poetic leadership began to grow.

Nowadays I spend my time connecting the dots. I work as a coach using creative approaches to leadership development and team building; I run performance based training events; I write, act, direct, pot and potter. I use creative approaches to help others (and, along the way, myself) to grow.

In a way, I have tried to write the leadership book that I craved years ago when I was starting out. One that speaks to my sense of self; to my love of mystery; to my intuitive style of sensing; to the somewhat odd way my mind works; to my need for human connection and authenticity - in short, to my inner poet.

Meeting the Leadership Challenge

Leaders and their followers are increasingly searching for meaning in the workplace. In a world of volatility, complexity and overwhelming data, many seek models of leadership that are more articulate and quiet; that link to the self and humanity; that bring meaning and creativity; that are comfortable with ambiguity. Yet we continue to work in environments that prioritise self-sufficiency and fast results; that reward directive styles of leadership. Many would argue that there is a widening gulf between what people want from their leaders, and what traditional modes of leadership succession and management development deliver.

Repeating old leadership practices when they aren't working is the managerial equivalent of shouting to be understood in a foreign country. If we keep doing what we always did, we'll keep getting what we always got. We need something different.

There is a plethora of authoritative advice about how one should lead, and a multitude of descriptions and definitions of leadership. Rather than trying to add to this canon, I am trying to provide a simple guiding light in the form of *a way of seeing* leadership.

The Poetic Leader

In this book, I suggest that leadership is (like) poetry. My premise is that:

- ❁ poetry has much in common with leadership and has something to offer on several levels
- ❁ poetry and poetic language can be powerful tools for leaders
- ❁ reading and understanding poetry can develop useful thinking skills for leaders
- ❁ using poetic devices and approaches (such as tone, rhythm, and narrative) can improve our leadership
- ❁ metaphor is useful not only in leadership but about leadership
- ❁ seeing leadership as a poetic activity can shift our relationship with our identity as leaders
- ❁ I offer up the idea of the poetic leader - someone whose leadership shares some of the characteristics of poetry and poetic writing. Poetic leadership is not about speaking in verse, but about a way of thinking and communicating that is beautiful, intelligent, complex, subtle, figurative, and questioning.

There are numerous approaches already that describe what the arts can bring to leadership, and how leadership is, for example, like conducting music, dancing or painting, or even more abstract ideas, like beauty. I am not aiming to compete with these; it is not an either/or argument. Many or all (or none) of these different approaches may land with you; they may complement each other.

As Rosamund and Ben Zander write in *The Art of Possibility*, "*The arts can break new ground here, bringing human consciousness to bear on these flows of product and capital, energising our interpersonal connections, and opening new doors for invention and practice*".[1]

The Approach

Using the fundamental building blocks of poetic writing, such as structure, form and the selection of language, I look at how poetry can guide the leader through choices.

I deal with some of the contentious areas of leadership, such as the balance between truth and performance, whether all leadership is performance however authentic, and the role of emotions at work.

I also explore specific leadership challenges, such as dealing with ambiguity, managing change and fostering innovation, and look at how a more poetic approach can shift the paradigm of these dilemmas.

Each chapter explores a particular facet of poetry or an element of poetic writing. There are also common threads and, perhaps, unexpected connections weaving throughout. You may notice resonances and echoes from one chapter to another.

In *Rhyme and Reason,* I am arguing a place for a particular kind of leadership – not by treatise or proof, but by showing a kind of truth and hoping to elicit a recognition. This showing, not telling, is what the poet does.

The book is part thesis, part guide, part stream-of-consciousness. I hope, above all, that you find it an inspiring look at the power and beauty of language.

A Poetic Tone

We often use metaphors to grasp complex abstract phenomena and see them in a different light. In employing metaphor here, I hope I might give you a different way to see your own leadership, and perhaps change your relationship with it.

This book is designed to be performative as well as descriptive of poetry. I have included examples of poetry, and drawn upon poetic constructs and devices. In this sense it may have both the tenor and the vehicle of the metaphor it employs. I find this internal consistency deeply pleasing.

Whilst I have illustrated some of the particular ways in which *I* think leadership is (or at least should be) poetic, the metaphor may spark more and different associations for you.

Leadership as Poetry - Is it True?

As we will see in Chapter 13, truth comes in many different guises. As Bob Dylan (a man who doesn't use his own name, nor sing in his own voice) allegedly said, *"All the truth in the world adds up to one big lie"*.

What does it mean to say that leadership is, or is *like*, poetry? Whether it is literally 'true' is not the point. The real question is, does it *seem* true? Does it contain a grain of truth - a small amount? Or even *the* grain - the kernel - of a truth? Something from which a bigger story might grow? William James suggested that any idea that helps us to deal, practically or intellectually, with reality, will meet the requirements of truth.

Another key question to ask might be whether this idea can foster praxis – that is, informed, committed action - by leaders themselves. Karl Marx argued that man must prove the truth of his thinking in practice, and that the point is not simply to understand the world but to change it. Praxis is creative - about acting upon or working with things - just as poetry (*poiesis*) is itself a making.

Here are some questions to help test the *truth* for you of this premise as you read:

- Does it resonate?

- Does it move you? What is your felt response to the suggestion that Leadership is a form of poetry?

- Is it useful? How does taking this idea help? Imagine playing with it, testing it out. Look at it. Turn it over. Put it away. Come back to it. Is there a germ of an idea there; of something of value?

- Does it somehow make you feel more content or less alone?

- Might it give you permission to use hidden skills in your leadership; skills that you have left at home?

- Might it give you a different set of tactics?

- What would it be to see yourself as a more poetic leader - might this facilitate better leadership; greater courage?

- If you are a poet, does this book say something to you about how you might also be a leader?

- What if this way of seeing could help poetry (and poets) to have greater influence in the business world; or raise the profile of poetry in leadership?

- If it can do any of these things, then perhaps it is 'true'.

How to Use It

This book is a discourse, not a proscriptive handbook. I hope you will use it to catalyse your own thoughts and reflections on the topics it raises. If you come to it expecting "*Ten easy steps to being a better manager*", you may be disappointed.

It is not a book that will tell you how you should be as a leader. It does not contain checklists or 'to-do' lists. There are numerous books and guides like that already, and their approaches work for many people. But if you are the kind of person who prefers to find new ways of seeing things, who tends to think in models and metaphors rather than 'how to's, then its *poetic* approach may work for you.

It is my sincere wish that *Rhyme & Reason* will help you, the reader, to find a deeper connection with who you are - and how you want to be - as a leader, whatever that means to you; that it will support you in taking the kinds of actions that will make your organisation (life, family, community) and the world a better place.

I would love to hear your responses to these ideas, and especially any ways you have used them in your own practice.

You can contact me at sam@differentdevelopment.com

You Reading This, Be Ready

Starting here, what do you want to remember?
How sunlight creeps along a shining floor?
What scent of old wood hovers, what softened
sound from outside fills the air?

Will you ever bring a better gift for the world
than the breathing respect that you carry
wherever you go right now? Are you waiting
for time to show you some better thoughts?

When you turn around, starting here, lift this
new glimpse that you found; carry into evening
all that you want from this day. This interval you spent
reading or hearing this, keep it for life -

What can anyone give you greater than now,
starting here, right in this room, when you turn around?

William Stafford

2

WHAT IS LEADERSHIP?

Leaders write organizational poetry

George Goens

An Alchemic Mix

In spite of considerable research and numerous books on the subject of leadership, we still have a limited understanding of what it is all about. Leadership might be one of those nebulous concepts or qualities that we recognise when we see, but is difficult to describe; to put our finger on.

My personal experience, and coaching work with a wide variety of individuals, brings me to this conclusion: that to be of value to the newly aspiring or the seasoned leader, definitions or descriptions of leadership must help them to identify not only what to do, but also how they want to be; how they might enact and embody leadership.

In this book I aim to describe a simple approach to leadership that I hope might provide some insight and perhaps serve as a Polaris to those trying to navigate their way.

One of the reasons that defining and understanding leadership is so slippery is that its alchemic mix is full of contradictions. Great leaders are said to demonstrate courage and reflection, bold yet careful choices, and a passionate but calming persona. People want their leaders to be decisive yet inclusive, to use their intellect whilst caring deeply, to have confidence and gravitas yet also be humble and approachable. Time and again great leadership requires not *either/or* but *both/and*. It demands that we can hold disparate ideas and possibilities to be true at once. It requires an ability to thrive in ambiguity and uncertainty.

Poetry makes an art form and discourse out of such contradiction and comparison. I believe it may hold a key.

What Do I Mean By Leadership?

In this book I try to outline not just what leaders *do*, but to illustrate what Leadership *is* as an entity. Although when we talk about leadership, we often think about people 'at the top', true leadership is often found in everyday situations. We all have leadership roles, in our lives, families and communities, and in the things that we create.

Leadership is especially noticeable in times of crisis, when ordinary people step up to take action and responsibility. I am focussing on *personal* leadership, not simply on the conferred authority that comes from having a certain position or job. Even leaders with formal authority must rely in large part on the impact of their behaviours and personae. Leaders earn trust and develop informal authority through their personal qualities and their actions; by being persuasive.

Extract from *To be of use*

I love people who harness themselves, an ox to a heavy cart,
who pull like water buffalo, with massive patience,
who strain in the mud and the muck to move things forward,
who do what has to be done, again and again.

Marge Piercy

In such personally-earned leadership, the ability to make sense of, and act in, situations that are out of the ordinary is key. In fact the essence of leadership savvy might be, as Jean Piaget suggested when describing intelligence, *knowing what to do, when you don't know what to do*, (provided of course that the leader then *does* it....!).

Leadership may be shared. It can also move. Much of what I say in relation to personal leadership will also apply to shared or distributed leadership, and to community settings.

Leadership Traits

Many leadership definitions and quotations focus on the perceived differences between *Leadership* and *Management*. Put simply, Leadership focusses on vision and what needs to be done, whilst management focuses on performance and how it is achieved.

Early management theory suggested that many of the characteristics of great leaders were inherent; that great leaders were born. It focused on the leader's role in relation to tasks; on getting people to do things. Over recent decades, the literature has drawn more heavily on sociological and psychological frameworks, and tends to suggest a range of leadership traits and skills that can be learned and developed; in other words, that leaders can be *made*. (See for example, Wall and Knights' work on *transpersonal* leadership.)

Another key shift in thinking has been away from hierarchical models, where leaders *tell* others what to do, towards influencing and engaging skills that *show* them how things might be. These skills are especially important in organisations needing distributed leadership, with a highly skilled workforce who are themselves required to lead and influence.

Leadership is a Relationship-based and Emotional Activity

Leadership is fundamentally personal. Great leaders inspire us to do our best by igniting our passion. Although we may try to explain their effectiveness in terms of strategy or vision, the reality is that leadership works though the emotions.

There are no leaders without followers. Leaders create connection and inspire people with contagious passion for their mission, and bring a sense of well-being to the workplace.

Leaders set out to inspire and influence the actions, beliefs and feelings of others, through their ability to use the tool of language to shape the understanding of others. Leaders need to master emotional intelligence in order to understand themselves and others. This requires self-awareness and learning, and a willingness to act or change in response to events and feedback.

Leadership is a Creative Act

Leaders are able to think and act creatively, and can focus on a reality that doesn't yet exist. Leaders create direction and momentum, and give meaning and purpose to work. Several authors, such as Benjamin Zander and Max De Pree, have likened leadership to the creative process, and draw parallels with the world of the arts.

Leadership is an Act of Courage

Leaders have to be courageous on a daily basis, often in spite of their own fear and uncertainty. They must take personal responsibility, and *show up* fully and authentically, as all of who they are. They must step into the void, the empty space that requires someone to lead, and make something happen. Above all, a leader must be willing to stand up and be seen.

Being a Leader

Studies of leadership tend to focus on the roles and functions of leaders, i.e. what it is that they do. However, exploring leaders' own experiences, or indeed the perspectives of those followers who have witnessed great (or not so great!) leadership, tends to elicit more information about how leaders *are*.

Leadership is an embodied activity - one that involves our minds, hearts and bodies - and authors are increasingly exploring what it means for a leader to *enact* their leadership role. Indeed, there are increasing numbers of leadership development courses that focus on physicality and the body, including the *Embodied Leadership* approach of Wendy Palmer and others.

The Night House

Every day the body works in the fields of the world
Mending a stone wall
Or swinging a sickle through the tall grass-
The grass of civics, the grass of money-
And every night the body curls around itself
And listens for the soft bells of sleep.

But the heart is restless and rises
From the body in the middle of the night,
Leaves the trapezoidal bedroom
With its thick, pictureless walls
To sit by herself at the kitchen table
And heat some milk in a pan.

And the mind gets up too, puts on a robe
And goes downstairs, lights a cigarette,
And opens a book on engineering.
Even the conscience awakens
And roams from room to room in the dark,
Darting away from every mirror like a strange fish.

And the soul is up on the roof
In her nightdress, straddling the ridge,
Singing a song about the wildness of the sea
Until the first rip of pink appears in the sky.
Then, they all will return to the sleeping body
The way a flock of birds settles back into a tree,
Resuming their daily colloquy,
Talking to each other or themselves
Even through the heat of the long afternoons.
Which is why the body-the house of voices-

Sometimes puts down its metal tongs, its needle, or its pen
To stare into the distance,

To listen to all its names being called
Before bending again to its labor.

Billy Collins

Making The Links

If you want to explore this topic further, there are a number of useful summaries of the canon of leadership theory. Some examples are given in the Bibliography.

In this book, I set out a new description of the *poetic leader*. We will be exploring different aspects of leadership in each chapter as we move through this book, and considering what poetry might bring to the different characteristics and challenges of leadership.

3

WHAT IS POETRY?

One demands two things of a poem. Firstly, it must be a well-made verbal object that does honor to the language in which it is written. Secondly, it must say something significant about a reality common to us all, but perceived from a unique perspective. What the poet says has never been said before, but, once he has said it, his readers recognize its validity for themselves.

W. H. Auden

The words poem and poetry derive from the Greek "ποίησις", poiesis, a "making" or "creating"). That is, a poem is a made thing: a creation; an artefact, emanating from an act of making. Denotatively, poetry is literary work in metrical form or verse. Its purpose is sometimes identified as being to excite pleasure by beautiful, imaginative thoughts. The word poetic is also given connotative meanings, such as the characteristics of beauty and spirit; of being elevated or sublime. Such characteristics extend to the poet herself, as one having the gift of imagination and eloquence. And we associate poetry with unconventionality (for example in the phrase poetic license), beauty (poetry in motion) and something that is right and fitting (poetic justice). Yet it would be hard to conjure in our minds the idea of a poem, based on these definitions.

Introduction to Poetry

I ask them to take a poem
and hold it up to the light
like a color slide

or press an ear against its hive.

I say drop a mouse into a poem
and watch him probe his way out,

or walk inside the poem's room
and feel the walls for a light switch.

I want them to waterski
across the surface of a poem
waving at the author's name on the shore.

But all they want to do
is tie the poem to a chair with rope
and torture a confession out of it.

They begin beating it with a hose
to find out what it really means.

Billy Collins

Poetry and things poetic tend to defy definition, and perhaps, as Billy Collins implies, we attempt to tie them down at our peril. Indeed, part of the impact of poetry may lie in its being simultaneously familiar and foreign; un-pin-downable.

Perhaps we recognise the poetic by how we respond to it, rather than by any innate, measurable qualities. Emily Dickinson's description of a poetic world in her poem *Dwelling in Possibility* conjures a landscape of opportunity and choice; of enlightenment yet secrecy. Poetry for Dickinson seemed, above all, a place of inspiration and soulfulness.

Nowadays, there are many different styles and forms of poetry. Sadly, many readers can be put off poetry at school, perhaps as a result of the limited range they are introduced to (the romantics may not appeal to adolescent tastes) or the overdone analysis of symbol and meaning that is sometimes brought to the English Literature syllabus. But saying 'I don't like poetry' is a bit like saying 'I don't like music' or ' I don't like paintings'. The canon is broad and contains the stylistic equivalents of everything from tribal chants to Puccini to Cage to Radiohead; from cave paintings to Michelangelo to Picasso to Richard Wright.

There are many books that explore the internal workings of poetry, and a growing number of books of work-related poems, either original or curated, that you may wish to explore. There are details of some of these resources in the Bibliography.

Later in this book we will look at the implications of poetry's characteristics for the trope at play - poetry as a way of seeing leadership. In this Chapter we will take a brief tour of the world of poetry, either as a reminder or an introduction, and review some of poetry's key features.

What Makes it Poetry ?

In a lecture at Cambridge University in 1933, A E Housman said that poetry is *"not the thing said, but a way of saying it"*. (Note the indefinite article).

There are certain aesthetic qualities and characteristics that we tend to associate with poetry (in the denotative sense) as opposed to prose, and with things *poetic*, including the poet herself (in the connotative sense).

Poetry is distinct in a number of ways. These include:

- a rhythmic quality
- rhyme or other repeating sounds
- heightened vocabulary - including symbolism and metaphor
- compression and efficiency
- the ability to convey emotion and meaning
- its reliance upon the line as a formal unit
- spaciousness of form - use of visual space, pauses and caesuras or line breaks
- freedom of syntax; breaking semantic rules

One of poetry's features is its ability to balance or fuse elements that are in tension, for example: sound and symbol; rhyme and rhythm; head and heart. These elements tap into different elements of our being - stimulating body, mind and soul; gut, heart and brain - at the same time.

Like great leadership, poetry connects with us emotionally, and our response to it can be powerful, unconscious and physical. Housman famously detailed this physical response, suggesting that the seat of our sensation in response to poetry is the pit of the stomach.

The Role of Poetry

Poetry is an ancient mode of human expression. It was used before language was written down to pass on social messages of religious, historical, and cultural significance to the next generation. It took the forms of hymns, incantations, and narrative poems, whose characteristic rhythms, rhymes and other sonic properties made it easier to remember. Early attempts to define poetry, such as by the ancient Greeks, focused on the uses of speech in rhetoric, drama, song and comedy.

Nowadays the canon of poetry encompasses many different modes, from celebratory to satiric, didactic to personal. A poet usually selects a form and accompanying tone that fits with the subject and purpose of the piece.

Although, since the time of the romantics, we have tended to associate poetic inspiration with the individual imagination, there is still an element of tribal association and shared experience in the recitation of popular poetry.

Historically, the poet's role was, as the Quakers say, to *'speak truth to power'* and to be a voice of social conscience in the face of corruption. Poets are able to touch hearts and minds, influencing mass opinion. This, of course, is why nefarious leaders and states will try to silence them. Yet a poet's impact is great because they also speak to the personal, through a medium well suited to celebrating each person's unique relationship with the world. Even when addressing issues of social and global significance, great poetry connects at an individual level, creating an intersecting Venn diagram of the personal and the political.

Poetic Language and Symbol

Powerful and often unusual use of language is a key distinguisher of poetic writing. The careful selection of words for conciseness and clarity is important in any writing, but poets must go further, considering each word's symbolic meaning and emotive qualities, its musical value, even its spacing on the page.

Poetry is often economical in its use of language. A strong poem can paint an evocative picture, disproportionate to the number of words it uses. Poetry pushes language to its utmost. Since effective communication is a vital leadership skill, poetry may have much to offer.

Poetry is often complex and subtle. Its use of devices of *meaning*, such as ambiguity, symbolism and irony often leaves a poem open to multiple interpretations. At the same time, metaphor and simile can create a resonance between otherwise disparate images, forming new mental and emotional connections.

Poetic writing is rich in symbol-laden words, and other poetic devices that can convey meanings or emotions hidden beyond the immediate words. It connects with our senses about abstract ideas and experiences; with what Keith Holyoak calls those *"intangible but achingly important concerns that may reduce prose to remote abstraction, at best, or nonsense, at worst."* [2] Poetic symbolism can expand a reader's imagination, and is a potent way of getting the unconscious mind on board. It is a skill well worth cultivating.

Sound

Alongside symbol, another fundamental element of poetry is sound; specifically the sound of the human voice, whose patterns we respond to emotionally. Whilst often read on the page, poetry remains a fundamentally vocal form - therein lies much of its power.

When well executed, attention to sound can produce combinations of rhythm and rhyme that sound almost inevitable once heard, and lend a poem congruence and gravitas.

We expect poetry to be pleasing or stimulating to hear or read, and at the same time, to reveal or tell us something interesting and new. A coherence between sense and sound is a characteristic of poetic writing. A poem makes some kind of proposition - a point of view or imaginative vision - and seeks to prove itself through the inviolability of its form.

The Book Of Tides

Like that, the old lass could switch into a ship's mast,
stood on that cliff, sea air wringing a swell of hips

and thighs out the rag of her skirt. Then, she was Ma,
dragging me through the plothery snicket again,
back to cottage in wait. Outside tinkled and strode.
Fishermen knocked, bags of whelks at the door,
trout like rainbows dandled from red hands. Aye,
the woman had a knack for the wind, knew it,
whisper to gale. She got weather the way a mute
woman, married forever, spoke to her husband
without breathing a word. I did not know if I'd live
magic too, if I'd ever piece together air, cut
through the bluster and blow in an ear to know
when to sigh a man home or wreck him en route.
Flick, flick, at licked pages in her big book of tides,
I watched her spit and tie the sky up, a snap
of her hair knotted into a handkerchief slipped
into the odd breast pocket. Some nights she stared
at wolves chasing the window, landlocked clouds
circled the house. The boats sailed right enough.
Fingers, curled in pockets, stroked our blood knots
like hungry birds listening for scraps of a heart.

Angela Readman

The Contract

Poetry does not exist in isolation but passes between the poet and the reader or listener. It evokes what Coleridge called 'a willing response', or what we might think of as a *followership*. Whilst there is no simple and universal distinction between prose and poetry, there does seem to be a psychological one. We read poetry with an expectation of creative expression because we associate the two. There is a linguistic contract between poet and reader, just as there is an organisational or social contract between leaders and the led.

4

POETRY AS A METAPHOR FOR LEADERSHIP

*To re-describe things through metaphor is to "leave out" and "carry-over"
meaning, to undergo a kind of dispossession of self, thing, place, and time and an
overcoming of both individualisms and dualities. Thus the meaningful expression
of the real is seen and experienced most directly in the endlessly creative activity
of art and music, rather than philosophy.*

Nietzsche

The Trope at Play!

A poem is a map of the world, or of a part of it. It is a representation; an imaginary construction. It is not the territory. It will hold different meaning, and uses, for different people. Yet a great poem may find and never leave us. It can guide us. It can *lead*.

Using metaphor and other linguistic devices, poetry enables us to describe a set of complex issues simply and elegantly. Choosing the right metaphor enables the poet to establish a congruence between subjective and objective realities; between topic and medium.

The trope of this book is the exploration of leadership through the metaphor of poetry. Metaphors establish a mindset that affects the way we see the world. They subtly influence what we believe and how we act. The metaphors we hear and use about leadership will set our expectations and inform the way we think and act as leaders. This being the case, we had best choose our metaphors wisely.

We tend to choose and use metaphors that resonate with us, and the metaphors we use tell much about the way we see the world. As a poet, the metaphor I use in this book makes sense to me, but it may not fit for everyone. Nevertheless, any different way of looking at the field of leadership can offer new insights. Your insights may of course be different to the ones I anticipate as I write. After all, metaphors have a habit of escaping the use for which they are intended.

Using poetry as a metaphor for leadership enables me to create imagery that has resonance and perhaps echoes your personal experience of leadership - your own and that of the leaders you admire. The metaphor provides us with a shorthand - a way of connecting with the truth on a more felt, intuitive level - and an idea of The *Poetic Leader*. It may not only offer a framework for thinking about leadership, but also tell us something about the here-and-now of communicating as a leader.

Postcards to Oregon

An angular figure tracks shapes
on the frost-packed shore. An Etruscan
town-plan waiting for tides to turn.

Sunday mornings rich with pilchard sauce.

First morning of October's rental,
ill-matched furnishings, remains of summer's
unexpired lease, front-lot rank
with shot garlic. Inside
a 1950s Frigidaire shudders into life.

I stamp postcards to Oregon and Seattle.

Between clearly articulated lanes and alleys
the angled figure sculpts earthworks,
drinks from a litre Evian bottle.

Third lines are invariably hardest.
I set aside the pen and seek out
an enamel coffee-pot, a means
of lighting gas, a passable cup.

Tarpaulined between runway and fence,
the small planes...

By noon, a new Atlantis at his feet,
this man possessed builds his castle
wilfully close to ebb and flow,
dredges a shin-deep moat
that fills as he digs; perfects
crenellated ramparts, sand drawbridges,
one tall keep, a kelp flag for pennant.

We build against oblivion.

A morning's drafts go in the flip-top bin.

Anne-Marie Fyfe

What is a Metaphor?

Aristotle believed a command of metaphor to be the mark of genius. A metaphor is an implied analogy in which one thing is compared or identified with another dissimilar thing. For example, describing a courageous person as having a "heart of a lion" or feelings such as "butterflies in the stomach". A sustained metaphor is known as an allegory.

A metaphor has two parts: the tenor and the vehicle. The tenor is the subject to which attributes are ascribed. The vehicle is the object whose attributes are borrowed.

> *All the world's a stage,*
> *And all the men and women merely players;*
> *They have their exits and their entrances;*

In this example from William Shakespeare's As You Like It, the world is compared to and given the attributes of a stage; the world is the tenor, and a stage is the vehicle; men and women is a secondary tenor, players is a secondary vehicle. So in this book, leadership is the tenor which we seek to understand with the help of another concept - poetry - as the vehicle.

A key symbol in an allegorical poem (such as a boat on the ocean) can serve to represent all the ideas we associate with it (courage, uncertainty, navigation, adventure). In turn, this may bring significance to previously unnoticed elements in the poem.

Rowing

> *I am rowing, I am rowing*
> *though the oarlocks stick and are rusty*
> *and the sea blinks and rolls*
> *like a worried eyeball,*
> *but I am rowing, I am rowing,*
> *though the wind pushes me back*

and I know that that island will not be perfect,
it will have the flaws of life.

Anne Sexton

Using metaphor to describe leadership as being *like* poetry enables me to explore its characteristics; to think about how we do the things that constitute being a leader. Broadening this to portray leadership as *being* poetry, makes it more concrete and personal; an entity in itself. A description of leadership *as* poetry gives some sense about what it is to lead. It enables us to explore the corpus of our leadership; a collection of leadership performances that add up to something poetic, rather than the canon of leadership theories.

How do Metaphors Work?

Metaphors play on the connotative properties of words. Although we give much of our attention to describing things in denotative terms, much of the expressiveness of language comes from connotation; the associations that a word usually brings to mind. Thus 'home' denotes the house where we live, but connotes security, cosiness, intimacy.

Metaphors are tools for making shifts of focus and of mind. They can build a bridge from the familiar to the unfamiliar, helping us to conceptualise that which is difficult to describe, and to notice new aspects of that which is well known. With metaphor, new knowledge unfurls. Metaphor can change the way we see something, sometimes forever. In time it can change the way we see. Yet it isn't literally 'true'. A metaphor connects in a way that 'makes sense' or 'rings true' but doesn't follow cause and effect logic. As Nietzsche said, *"On every metaphor you ride to every truth"*.

Metaphors contain implicit conceptualisations, or ways of seeing the world, that can illuminate in ways that other, more concrete, descriptions may not. The interplay between two separate ideas achieves a kind of cross-mapping.

However, only certain aspects of the target domain tend to be focused on in metaphors. The metaphor (e.g. the man is a lion) frames our understanding of the man in a distinctive yet partial way. By highlighting certain aspects of the target domain, other competing aspects are hidden. The metaphor provides a filter; it shows an issue in a particular light.

Metaphor always creates distortions. It uses evocative images to create *constructive falsehoods* which, if taken literally or to an extreme, would become absurd. Metaphor invites us to see similarities but ignore differences. This is one reason why metaphor can be so powerful when used to create shared understanding and consensus. Metaphor also stays open to change.

Metaphor is not simply a rhetorical device. The use of metaphor implies a way of thinking and a way of seeing that pervades how we understand our world. Linguistic research suggests that people use a metaphor every 10 to 25 words. Far from being rhetorical frills, metaphors are at the very heart of how we think, according to James Geary in *I Is an Other*. Researchers George Lakoff and Mark Johnson, too, in *Metaphors We Live By*, suggest that metaphor exerts a formative influence on science, online language, and even mass political opinion.

Uses of Metaphor in Organisations

Since organisational theory, like all theory, is based on implicit images or metaphors, it is inherently incomplete and biased. No single theory can provide a perfect or all-purpose point of view. However, it can sometimes offer a new one.

If, as leaders, we can develop the art of using metaphor, we may be able to find fresh ways of seeing, understanding, and shaping the situations that we want to manage. Metaphor in organisations can be used both as a tool for improving communication and engagement (discourse theory), and as a way of understanding organisational culture (cognitive theory).

From a discourse theory perspective, metaphors can be positioned and used within specific conversations by the leader to manage their own interests in social interaction. Metaphors form an important element in organisational storytelling. To have best effect, we must find a metaphor that will resonate with the specific audience with whom we are speaking.

Metaphors are also a powerful tool for understanding leadership. Metaphors are usually contextual and cultural. They reflect the values of the speaker (and often their audience) and can provide valuable insight into organisational culture or the inner thoughts of an individual. For example, at work you may hear an individual say 'bring out the big guns'. This figure of speech may reveal an inner perception of work as being like war.

Early metaphors of leadership tended to emphasise traits most commonly associated with powerful men. Later, alternatives such as sporting or factory metaphors emerged. As our thinking about leadership has developed, other disciplines have informed our leadership metaphors, for example the arts and spirituality.

Overhearing and understanding an organisation's metaphors can provide insights to the subtle beliefs and values shared by the people who work there - work is a zoo; life is a bitch; the hospital is a machine; marketing is fluffy. Such insights are of great value to leaders and those (such as organisational development practitioners) who may be working with them on any change agenda.

Climbing Above Rongbuk Monastery

A golden spire
draped with prayer-flag rainbows
and Qomolangma
burnished by summer snows

Point the way upward
beyond the human world—

the air gets thinner,
the end of the earth draws close.

Nothing but ice,
and rock, and wind, and sky—
life colors have vanished,
even the green of moss.

Gasping for breath
I crawl on hands and knees—
between bare stones
a purple blossom grows.

Keith Holyoak

Metaphor in Leadership Development

Whatever metaphor you have (for life, or work or home) will colour how you see things, will surface in your behaviours and the words you use, and will influence your interactions with others. Metaphor is therefore often a crucial part of coaching and other leadership development conversations. Understanding a person's metaphors can provide crucial insights to their inner feelings, memories, beliefs and values. It can provide an opportunity not only to understand what may be driving their actions, but to support the embedding of more helpful metaphors. This is especially true of metaphors about the individual themselves, and how they relate to the world.

Just as there is more than one language or style of leadership, there is undoubtedly more than one metaphor that works. The best metaphor for you may relate to the sector you work in, your gender, or the particular organisational circumstances you find yourself in. Above all, your own leadership metaphor should align with the kind of leader you want to be.

Because metaphors of self extend across specific scenarios, they lend themselves particularly well to cross-discipline confidence building. For example, gaining a sense of ourselves as able in one field, will have positive ramifications in another. This is especially true of any intervention that gives us a felt sense or clear image of success, and is an approach we use extensively in the leadership development programmes at *Different Development*.

Summary

In this book I have set out a simple metaphor for leadership that I hope you can carry with you. There are no checklists to refer to, to see if you are 'doing it right'. Perhaps all that you'll need (and I hope want) to do is to keep reading and, maybe, writing poetry.

In the remaining chapters, I articulate a place for poetic leadership, and explore different aspects of poetry and leadership, drawing parallels between them, to show what we might gain from leading poetically.

5

A PLACE FOR POETRY

The grand power of poetry is its interpretative power; by which I mean, not a power of drawing out in black and white an explanation of the mystery of the universe, but the power of so dealing with things as to awaken in us a wonderfully full, new, and intimate sense of them.

Matthew Arnold

What is Poetry For?

Why should we give attention to poetry. Is it 'relevant'? How might poetry and the poetic earn a place in our crowded lives, organisations and minds? What does it have to offer to busy leaders?

In a world where creativity and innovation are key differentiators, where people are increasingly looking for meaning in their work, and where clarity and truth can be hard to find, many believe that the arts have something to offer.

To live is miracle enough

To live at all is miracle enough.
The doom of nations is another thing.
Here in my hammering blood-pulse is my proof.

Let every painter paint and poet sing
And all the sons of music ply their trade;
Machines are weaker than a beetle's wing.

Swung out of sunlight into cosmic shade,
Come what come may the imagination's heart
Is constellation high and can't be weighed.

Nor greed nor fear can tear our faith apart
When every heart-beat hammers out the proof
That life itself is miracle enough.

Mervyn Peake, in *The Glassblower*, 1950

Violinist Miha Pogacnik argues that experiencing a masterpiece can *"gradually call forth new capabilities in people. People learn to see and listen in new ways, which may enable them to suddenly see complicated social constellations in new ways and also to find new ways of resolving them."* [3]

Certainly business requires new approaches and transformative thinking, and the whole field of Arts in Business has grown in the last decade. Within this field, poetry seems to be an especially accessible and effective medium, perhaps because it is language based. Whilst intensive work in any of the arts is likely to improve emotional and intuitive abilities, poetry in particular also helps to develop linguistic skills. Poetry uses the same communication channels we use for planning, decision making and engagement in the business world, but uses them in a special way. Reading poetry opens up new thinking spaces, and develops skills that can help us to see and think differently.

In the foreword to *What Poetry Brings to Business* by Clare Morgan, businessman-poet John Barr argues that business and poetry are more alike than either knows. Although the businessman and poet delight in making sense of things respectively in the external and internal world, "*The business of both is to create order out of a chaotic universe.*" [4]

Poetry is being brought into the boardrooms, training spaces and marketing strategies of a wide range of organisations, including numerous corporations (such as Coudal Partners and Boeing), West Point military academy and different healthcare settings. It has been used for employee engagement, for marketing, for holding the sense of a meeting or a vision, for creating shifts in understanding.

We use poetry in a variety of personal and organisational development approaches at my own company. Others working in this field include Martin Best, Judy Sorum Brown, David Whyte and William Ayot.

Of course, poetry won't go down well with everyone. There is a bit of the *Marmite* syndrome about it. A love/hate relationship with poetry is nothing new. Both Socrates and Plato were famously anti-poet. As indeed, those in authority in many times, places and regimes have been fearful of poets and the truth they might bring.

Plato identified poets (and storytellers) as dangerous fellows who put unreliable knowledge into the heads of children, and said that they would be subject to strict censorship in The Republic, lest their persuasive words or *mousa* should lead to great upheavals of social custom and law. He saw dramatic poetry as mimesis (imitative of 'sensible' things) rather than digesis (rational description). Socrates, too, hated the indirection he found in poetry, seeing it as '*Charm and Magic*'. This, of course, is also its strength. My experience tells me that most people are engaged and moved by the whole story, not simply the facts.

In 1985, Governor of New York Mario Cuomo echoed a Socratean view of poetry, suggesting that whilst he might campaign in poetry, he would *govern in prose*. Socrates and Cuomo both seem to undervalue the precision and specificity that poetry brings to language, image, nuance and tone.

Whilst poetry may have a mixed reception in organisations, in those where it has been championed there are numerous success stories; it seems to resonate and to help leaders in unexpected ways. Some pundits argue that poets will become increasingly commonplace within the heart of our corporations. Whether true or not, it is certainly worth leaders themselves developing some of the skills of the poet.

Ideas Over Facts

In his 1880 text *The Study of Poetry*, Matthew Arnold wrote fervently of poetry's ability to address themes that seem current now: "*Our religion has materialised itself in the fact, in the supposed fact; it has attached its emotion to the fact, and now the fact is failing it. But for poetry the idea is everything; the rest is a world of illusion, of divine illusion. Poetry attaches its emotion to the idea; the idea is the fact.*" [5]

I. A. Richards wrote with similar prescience in *Science and Poetry* in 1926, arguing that the facts and ideas then held as true may be as dangerously inadequate as views on hygiene, gravity and the shape of the earth once were. He suggested that life for the average educated man was becoming more complex and intricate, his desires and needs more varied and more apt to conflict, and that to live *reasonably* was more difficult than ever. Richards stressed that *"to live reasonably is not to live by reason alone - the mistake is easy and, if carried far, disastrous - but to live a way of which reason, a clear full sense of the whole situation, would approve."*

Like Coleridge before him, Richards believed that the importance which has been in the past assigned to poetry - the fact that it has captured the hearts and minds of people across the globe for thousands of years - needed to be *accounted for*, whether we conclude rightly so or not.

Utility & Praxis

The modern work environment places great emphasis on measurable outputs and return on investment. In this context it may be difficult to quantify the impact of poetry. Yet this may be missing the point.

The debate between those who look for economic impact, and those who appeal to the pursuit of knowledge in its own right, replicates an enduring dichotomy between utilitarianism and romanticism. There is an age-old debate about art and its function. Must art serve a utilitarian or didactic purpose, or is its intrinsic value (*Art for Art's Sake*) enough? Is every great work of art *autotelic* - complete in itself?

This debate, and the associated quarrel about the relative values of art and rational knowledge (or science) has been played out by Aristotle and Socrates in ancient Greece; by Jeremy Bentham and Samuel Taylor Coleridge in the 1800s, and carries on today in boardrooms, journals, the poetry press and, no doubt, in many living rooms too. It may still be true that we are born either a Platonist or an Aristotelian, a Napoleonist or a Tolstoyan, a stoic or an epicurean.

While rationalists encourage us to draw divisions, and to expel poets from the republic of discourse, other schools of philosophy seek to access a more ancient wisdom; one in which assertion and imagination are not divided. The discourse of post-structural philosophers such as Hélène Cixous and Roland Barthes aspires to span poetry and philosophy; performance and thought. Bringing a poetic lens to leadership performance is one way of bridging this gap.

> *There's nothing sentimental about a machine.*
>
> *A poem is a small (or large) machine made out of words. When I say there's nothing sentimental about a poem, I mean that there can be no part that is redundant. Prose may carry a load of ill-defined matter like a ship. But poetry is a machine which drives it, pruned to a perfect economy.*
>
> William Carlos Williams

As William Carlos Williams describes, poems, like machines, do whatever they are designed to do. They have a purpose. The work done by a poem is the effect it produces in the reader's mind. It is elegantly efficient in this work, both in its use of words and of our time. It goes deep, fast. Williams also argued that a poem should also be a *field of action*; that we should choose to write about things of importance, to select our purpose with care. Poetry, as a made thing, makes the bridge between doing and knowing, neither of which have validity or sufficiency without the other.

Universal Truths

Part of poetry's relevance may be its universality and its enduring nature. It enables us to see ourselves and current circumstances as part of a continuum, a community extending across history. Philosophers like Nietzsche and Schopenhauer describe how art helps us to set aside our sense of individuality and self, and to see life directly through timeless ideas.

As Aristotle argued, ethical knowledge comes from perceptions of the particular (yet universally true) not the general. This is key to what makes poetry useful, and, ultimately, dangerous. Poetry is argument by example rather than abstract reasoning. According to Elizabethan courtier Sir Philip Sidney, author of *An Apology for Poetry*, poetry surpasses history because it tells us how life ought to be and surpasses philosophy because it gives us the particular example. It works by connecting the universal with the personal or individual; with a significant moment. Its fulcrum is the place where public meets private; what Shelley called *'the electric life'*.

Extract from *The Music-makers*

We are the music-makers,
And we are the dreamers of dreams,
Wandering by lone sea-breakers,
And sitting by desolate streams.
World-losers and world-forsakers,
Upon whom the pale moon gleams;
Yet we are the movers and shakers,
Of the world forever, it seems.

Arthur O'Shaughnessy

Waking Us Up

Poetry can move and shake us. It can wake up our senses, which are over-stimulated by the constant noise of modern society and at the same time under-stimulated by lack of silence, pauses, and concentration. It can sharpen our senses too. Poetry stretches our minds. It helps us to say or understand difficult truths.

Poetry also triggers the emotions, aligning the power of the mind with the power of the heart. This is a key dimension in poetic leadership.

Poet David Whyte believes that the tradition of poetry is of a space where we as individuals can meet the world around us. In *The Heart Aroused*, he explores the state of the soul in the corporate workplace and shows how poetry can help people to identify and articulate what is important to them. Given that we spend a large proportion of our waking hours at work, it is vital to create environments in which we and others can thrive.

Outside of the workplace, people operate with free thought and self leadership; they make important investment decisions, multi-task, build relationships, make plans and have difficult conversations. These skills are not entirely abandoned at the office or factory door, but they are often under-used. Effective leaders cultivate these skills and provide people with opportunities for self leadership, creativity and innovation. They enable people to take on the leadership of their time and the stuff (things, ideas, relationships, conversations) that they personally create.

100%

We few, we happy few, we band of brothers and sisters,
We riskers of life and limb, or, at the very least, of our pockets,
Our wallets or our popular social standing, for all that we believe in,
We stand together.

We believers, in a time of unbelieving,
We grievers, making safe spaces for grieving,
We, authentic, in a world of slick deceiving,
We, holding integrity, not exploiting, not thieving,
We stand together.

We asking questions in a land of the unquestioning,
We, questing, while laurelled heads are resting,
We, hosting, as freely as guesting,
We teaching when we've been instructed to be testing,
We, pointing out the ridiculous, not just pointless jesting,
We switching off the TV, doing something more interesting,
We, deeply, communally, sustainably investing,

We recognising, honouring, counting and owning
Our own and each other's blessings,
We stand together.

We few, we happy few, we band of brothers and sisters,
We resisters of manipulation, we facilitation assisters,
We men, women and children of action,
Just getting on with our own revolution,
Which will not be televised
Will not be captured on I-phones
Will not be set loose on you-tube.
This is it happening here. We are it.
We stand together.

We, the music makers and we, the dreamers of dreams,
We, the Hopers, Komedians and Jubilee Librarians,
We, free-rangers, forest rangers, lone rangers, power rangers,
We mentors, mentees, mentalists and meant-to-bes,
We sun-kissed, clench-fist, anarchist activists,
We cyclers, recyclers, freecyclers, menstrual cyclers,
We tree-huggers, ear-muggers, levellers and diggers
And all of society's constructors, deconstructors and reconstructors,
Lover, warrior, magician and our own blessed majesties,
We stand together.

We few, we happy few, we band of brothers and sisters,
We poets and masters of these amazing ceremonies,
Who heard, in a furious flash, the message
And knew, in that moment, that we had a message to share,
We stand together.

We, separated painfully at birth from the planet
And, sometime in childhood, cut off from humanity
And, as soon as we thought that we had it,
Split off from ourselves,

Half dreaming of heaven, half walking in hell,
Or three-quarters woman and one-quarter man,
Or 7 parts coping and 3 parts mad,
While 8 out of 10 cats don't give a damn about the other 2,
We cats do!

We are the 99%,
And, what's more, we remember that story about the one lost sheep.
We're looking out for you.
We stand together.

Michael James Parker

Not Just *Poems*

In the writing and current thinking about poetry as an art in business, the focus thus far has been on poems as made artefacts (that is, on poetry in its denotative sense). Certainly poems are used to good effect in organisational development work, and by individual leaders, and there are numerous examples of relevant and powerful poems throughout this book. However, I believe that thinking more broadly about the poetic qualities of leadership adds another dimension to this theme. We will explore this in the chapters to follow.

6

THE POETIC LEADER

Lord, what an organ is human speech when employed by a master

Mark Twain

Introduction

What might it mean to lead poetically? To be a poetic leader? And why does it matter? Why do we need creative or poetic leaders?

Poetry deals in the currencies of passion and truth; currencies that are also vital in successful leadership. Leadership is deeply personal and rife with challenges and dilemmas that must be met with imagination, courage and wit. These common currencies have led numerous leaders to seek inspiration and solace in poetry, and writers such as the likes of George Goens and Clare Morgan to explore how poetry might be helpful to individual leaders and to organisations.

The Contract

A word from the led

And in the end we follow them -
not because we are paid,
not because we might see some advantage,
not because of the things they have accomplished,
not even because of the dreams they dream
but simply because of who they are:
the man, the woman, the leader, the boss,
standing up there when the wave hits the rock,
passing out faith and confidence like life jackets,
knowing the currents, holding the doubts,
imagining the delights and terrors of every landfall;
captain, pirate, and parent by turns,
the bearer of our countless hopes and expectations.
We give them our trust. We give them our effort.
What we ask in return is that they stay true.

William Ayot

There is a growing recognition that traditional styles of leadership are no longer adequate for the complex and busy world we inhabit. Exponents of the 'new' leadership styles spotlight similar and overwhelmingly *personal* features. There is now evidence that these characteristics are not only inherently admirable, but that they have an impact on performance; on staff and customer satisfaction and on outcomes, including financial. Society now aspires to develop and reward leaders who are different.

Key components of the new leadership include:

- great communication, that speaks to us as individuals
- honesty and authenticity
- engagement rather than direction of people
- the ability to balance workload and pace
- emotional intelligence
- an ability to challenge assumptions
- an ability to manage ambiguity and make links between seemingly unconnected things
- an aesthetic sensibility, including economy of words and effort
- bringing meaning to people's work
- finding and telling powerful stories
- balancing inherent tensions, for example being, at once, visionary yet realistic; corporate yet personal; dispassionate yet engaged.

Many of these characteristics, along with a both-and quality, can be found in poetry. Exploring this link provides a useful window onto what it means to lead in these times; how individuals might develop a greater sense of their own leadership essence, and practice the skills, behaviours and choices needed to embody a poetic way of leading.

In the Chapters that follow we will explore some specific characteristics and devices of poetic writing, and how they might inform our leadership practice. For example, we will look at language in Chapters 7 and 8; at honesty and performance in Chapter 13; at link-making and ambiguity in Chapter 17; and at courage and trust in Chapter 19.

For now, let us consider some of the associated connotations of poetry and how these relate to the leadership canon by exploring some characteristics of a 'poetic leadership'.

Communication

According to EB White, a poet is a person who "*lets drop a line that gets remembered in the morning*". Leaders too are judged on the impact of their communication. Effective leaders communicate clearly, concisely (and emotionally). In his treatise on poetry, Plato argues a central and controversial principle, that good speech, good accord, good shape and good rhythm follow upon *goodness of character*. Good speech may not be enough alone to identify goodness of character, but in the leadership mix it is a vital component; a necessary if insufficient condition. And this sense of right and good is echoed in the connotation implied by *poetic justice*.

Unique and Individual

Being a 'leader' is a personal métier. It flows from an individual's qualities and actions. A leader's tone and voice is distinctive. Similarly, although much writing is not autobiographical, it nevertheless always contains the experiential DNA of the writer.

To lead effectively, we must be willing to be seen; to have our unique and authentic voice heard. To stand up as a part of our community and our landscape.

Silver Star

To be a mountain you have to climb alone
and accept all that rain and snow. You have to look
far away when evening comes. If a forest
grows, you care; you stand there leaning against
the wind, waiting for someone with faith enough
to ask you to move. Great stones will tumble
against each other and gouge your sides. A storm
will live somewhere in your canyons hoarding its lightning.

If you are lucky, people will give you a dignified
name and bring crowds to admire how sturdy you are,
how long you can hold still for the camera. And some time,
they say, if you last long enough you will hear God;
a voice will roll down from the sky and all your patience
will be rewarded. The whole world will hear it: "Well done."

William Stafford

We must also be willing to show our own vulnerability; to be, at the same time, courageous and fearful. Our strongest connections with others will go deep, through our own experience; through our privacy. Yet our point of view must be broad, not egocentric.

Like great artists, effective leaders give us perspective and cultivate an appreciation of our world, ourselves, and our choices. The best of them can change our lives. They invigorate, comfort and motivate us. They forge a sense of community and bring us closer together by providing a forum for shared experiences.

The Place of Charisma

One of the tensions a leader has to manage is expressing her strong and clear persona without being domineering.

Charisma (literally a divinely conferred gift) is key in how we look at leadership, but this is rocky terrain. We use the term to refer to the qualities - the skills, personality and presence - of particular individuals, often self-appointed leaders who are followed by others in a crisis. Whilst charismatic leadership can be both beautiful and powerful, it carries with it a particular ego-centricity. Charisma is open to abuse by the ill-motivated leader, and can be destructive, including of a follower's sense of self and identity. We can all think of charismatic yet ultimately destructive leaders. Engagement with extreme versions of charisma can veer into the soul-destroying, witnessed in the 'shadow side' of charismatic power recounted by writers such as Manfred Kets de Vries.

Leaders have ethical and moral responsibilities to use their influence well. They have the power to cast shadow or light on a part of the world and onto the lives of those who inhabit it. An awareness of our dark side is vital, and the arts, including poetry, may help us to inquire into it.

Extract from Sonnet 94

The summer's flower is to the summer sweet,
Though to itself it only live and die,

But if that flower with base infection meet,
The basest weed outbraves his dignity:

For sweetest things turn sourest by their deeds;
Lilies that fester smell far worse than weeds.

William Shakespeare

As we shall see in Chapter 14, much poetry does not *tell* but *shows*. The poetic leader will do the same. In this sense they may not be classically charismatic. They will have a strong and authentic style and tone, but their own individual point of view will not dominate. Rather than having an egotistic or narcissistic focus, they help to bring meaning to a wider discourse, and keep it accessible by enabling others to make it their own. Such leaders act as vehicles for the hopes and aspirations of others; they serve.

Leading Quietly

Much poetry has a quietness about it, and this is a quality increasingly revered in our leaders today. Although often it is the characteristics of ego (such as self belief, focus and a desire to succeed) that get us to a leadership position, in the long run ego can prevent us from being effective and truly great leaders. Sustainable leadership success is about allowing others to achieve and flourish; ultimately, we can only advance if we cede control and put our employees first.

This is echoed in the artistic process. As German philosopher Martin Heidegger says, "*It is precisely in great art .reu.. that the artist remains inconsequential as compared with the work, almost like a passageway that destroys itself in the creative process for the work to emerge*". [6]

It is an important part of the leadership role to create an environment that enables others to communicate in a clear open and straightforward way. The leader must see as well as *being* seen; they must have a voice that listens. Indeed, the Greek Philosopher Diogenes (412 BC-323 BC) argued that "*We have two ears and one tongue so that we would listen more and talk less*".

Rather than poetic leaders believing that they have all the answers, they find out what is important through reflection and in dialogue with others, much as a writer will use the act of writing to gain understanding of their subject (or, indeed, of themselves). Burghild Nina Holzer follows this personal thread in her tender journal *Between Heaven & Earth*, saying "*Talking to paper is talking to the divine. Paper is infinitely patient. Each time you scratch on it, you trace part of yourself, and thus part of the world, and part of the grammar of the universe."* [7]

Authentic and Integrated

Authenticity is part of the current zeitgeist in a number of arenas, and leadership is no exception. Authenticity and integrity are qualities often cited about successful leaders, especially by their direct reports and other staff. Researchers such as Avolio and Gardner [8] suggest that authentic leadership offers a competitive advantage, and enables an organisation to achieve persistently high performance and growth. At its heart is a clear link between the leader's ethical values and their behaviour. Authenticity is built over time, as followers perceive the degree to which a leader is consistent, reliably takes certain positions, and behaves in line with organisational and societal culture and norms.

Whilst authenticity depends on the eye of the beholder, *integrity* is sensed most strongly by the individual as a feeling or state of being whole or *undiminished*. In great poetry, too, there is a sense of integrity and fit. We will explore the leadership qualities of integrity and authenticity in Chapter 9.

Beauty

There is no doubt that the word *poetic* has overtones of beauty. Leadership too has been suggested to have an aesthetic quality. For example Donna Ladkin describes leadership as an embodied activity and suggests that certain individuals lead *beautifully*. The idea of beautiful leadership also, importantly, implies a leadership that is truthful.

Most concepts of beauty include an association of form and function along with purpose, balance, measure or economy, and feeling - ideas that are as relevant in leadership as they are in the arts.

Performance

Deliberate or not, all leadership behaviours and communications involve an element of performance. There is considerable debate about the role of performance in leadership, and the extent to which we are always performing - and whether such performance is inevitably inauthentic.

Many aspects of leadership emulate the performing arts. As leaders, we must think not only of *what* we say, but of *how* we say it, including the use of gesture, tone, and symbol to convey meaning. It is this performative dimension of leading which moves the hearts and minds of followers. As in poetry, the language of effective leadership is especially rich in gesture, tone and symbol.

Courage and Truth

Poets have a reputation for seeing society and the world through a new lens; of speaking difficult truths, carving a courageous role for themselves. As leaders too we need to speak up. Leadership means making bold and often unpopular decisions. It involves creating ground-breaking but tradition-defying ideas. It may demand being repeatedly rejected before prevailing. Leadership takes courage.

One of the most courageous, and ultimately lonely, things that the strong leader must do is to ask difficult questions and to speak uncomfortable truths. In this regard effective leaders have more than a little of the poet about them. Traditionally it has been the maverick, the heretic, the poet, who challenges the established order. To adapt and survive in an uncertain and volatile world, organisations need to ask themselves difficult questions. In support of this quest, good leaders must adopt some of the stances of the poet, as well as seeking out the counsel of those (both within and without their organisation) who are able to tell them the truth. We explore the qualities of poetic truth in Chapter 13.

Story and Meaning

Much poetry has a strong storytelling component, from grandly orchestrated sagas, such as Beowulf, to the quieter and more personal narrative of lyrical poetry.

Leaders are storytellers too. They help to bring meaning to people's work, to make connections, both intellectual and emotional, and to create a shared organisational narrative. This works at both the public and the personal levels. We look at poetic and leadership narrative in Chapter 15.

Working at the Edge

Effective leaders have a track record of success, yet are honest about their failures. They work at the edge of their ability, constantly striving for greater things, and resilient enough to be able to move on and learn from mistakes. They take risks. They improvise.

Professor David Morley of Warwick University, describes this place of not knowing as a moving edge, where previous knowledge, guesswork and intuition combine, and, like a piece of poetry, are imagined and written into being.[9] We will explore this further in Chapter 18.

Vision

A key characteristic of leadership is the ability to develop a shared picture of the future we seek to create. Leaders must be visionaries. Such vision can encourage experimentation and innovation, and foster a sense of the long-term, which is fundamental to a vibrant and sustainable organisation.

Leaders who focus on vision and potential rather than on other's perceived shortcomings will build an organisation where people learn and grow. Such leaders *inspire* (or breathe life into) their organisations.

poet breathe now –

because it's the last thing you'll ever do for yourself.

*poet breathe now because there's a fire inside you that needs oxygen to
burn and if you don't run out of breath you're gonna run out of time*

Adam Gottlieb

A Daily Practice

Much of our leadership impact is in the quotidian, the quietly curated; not in
the grand gesture or set-piece of the board meeting or staff consultation. If we
find our authentic leadership voice, it will be noticed not only in how we lead,
but in how we live. And moving towards our goal isn't a singular activity. In her
book, *Composing a Life*, Mary Catherine Bateson contends, that "*our aesthetic
sense, whether in works of art or in lives, has over-focused on the stubborn struggle
toward a single goal rather than on the fluid, the protean, the improvisatory. We
see achievement as purposeful and monolithic, like the sculpting of a massive tree
trunk that has first to be brought from the forest and then shaped by long labor to
assert the artist's vision, rather than something crafted from odds and ends, like a
patchwork quilt, and lovingly used to warm different nights and bodies.*"[10] In my
experience, crafting a poem is always like this; snippets of ideas and words,
images and sounds, woven together. A poetic leadership will be personally
crafted. It will have something of the improvised and the homespun about it.

Needling *
For Jane Carson Davies

Between Her Woman's Fingers And Her Thumb
the needle sits; fine as a farthing piece;
And with an eye for detail, sharp, it does
a little digging, sometimes splinters, things
stuck down the back of things, but mostly it
joins up, pulls in, embroiders, following
the motifs of our Grandmothers. Now she
will tessellate; in transatlantic quilts
is caught between her mother's Celtic craft
and her new world pursuit; the tacking lines
and stitching holes a message home in Morse,
or clues in Braille to run her fingers over.
Between her woman's fingers and her thumb
the needle sits. She'll punctuate with it.

Beth Somerford
* After *Digging* By Seamus Heaney

Developing Poetic Leadership

The idea of a *poetic leadership* represents a synthesis of the qualities I focus on in my leadership development work, whether in one-to-one coaching, training, team building or strategy work. I include some examples of development approaches in the individual chapters that follow.

7

The Language of Leadership

Poetry is ordinary language raised to the Nth power.
Poetry is boned with ideas, nerved and blooded with emotions,
all held together by the delicate, tough skin of words

Paul Engle

Speaking Poetically

Many writers on leadership suggest an important role for particular styles of language in leaders' effectiveness, and offer instructions to help leaders improve their communication style and vocabulary. I believe that bringing elements of the poetic to our use of language will give us greater impact, make us better leaders, and be more deeply satisfying.

In this chapter we look at some of the characteristics of poetic language, to help inform an instinctive sense of powerful leadership language. We also consider how the language that leaders use can offer a window on the experience of leading. We will take a peek.

What is Language?

Language consists not only of the words we choose, but of the way they are put together. The impact of our language is made up of vocabulary, style, tone, symbol and sound. Our body language, too, includes equivalent elements; our posture and gestures are vital in the impression we create for others, in the creation of gravitas. As linguistic chameleons, we change the way we speak depending on who we are speaking to, choosing different words, inflexions, pitches and volumes to fit the situation.

Words are powerful, emotive and evocative. They say everything about us. Beyond our cultural background and education, they tell others what is important to us, how we think, and what we want. Whether consciously or not, we choose the words we use, and it is important to be aware of the impact they have.

Language is power[ful]. This is why dictators often try to silence its most skilled exponents.

> "... *many wearing rapiers are afraid of goose-quills and dare scarce come thither.*"
> Rosencrantz, in *Hamlet,* by William Shakespeare

A rich vocabulary, full of texture and colour, is both nourishing and surprising. We are stimulated by hearing an unusual way of saying something.

Our everyday communication is tinged with inflexion and meaning. It is easier to hear these hues in the spoken word, but important to attend to the impact of tone of our written communications too, as they are semi-permanent, and ripe for misunderstandings.

Successful leadership language

We recognise great leaders in part from the language they use. Leadership language is different. Whilst managers pay attention to getting things done, leaders concentrate on the meaning of events and decisions; they are sensitive to language. The language of leadership is colourful, peppered with symbolism and metaphor, laced with examples, and imprinted with a clear message or call for action. Effective leaders use appropriate metaphors and symbols for ideas and ideals.

A leader must take big, new and wonderful ideas and make them comprehensible. Great leadership language can speak in headlines without drowning in the details. It avoids abstractions such as 'culture' and the new verb 'performance-manage', and clichés such as 'the elephant in the room' and 'our people are our most important asset'. It makes the message important and personal to the listener. It doesn't deny problems, but reframes them as challenges rather than crippling obstacles.

Great leaders do not need to prove their status by using management speak or clever abbreviations. They don't need to try that hard. Instead, a leader's vocabulary should be clear, reverent, engaging and harmonious.

A poetic example of such clear speaking can be found in William Carlos Williams' simple poem, *This Is Just To Say*:

I have eaten

the plums

that were in

the icebox

and which

you were probably

saving

for breakfast

Forgive me

they were delicious

so sweet

and so cold

Imagine some of the possible management speak alternatives, including:

- ☼ the impersonal - "the plums have been eaten"
- ☼ the rules-based - "plums should be stored at room temperature"
- ☼ the over factual - "on 95% of mornings, I don't eat plums",
- ☼ the vague - "someone has eaten the plums", or
- ☼ the blame-shifting - "if you hadn't left your plums in the icebox, I wouldn't have eaten them"

The Power of Poetic Language

There is particular strength in the language of poetry. Philosopher Hans-Georg Gadamer claims that whereas *'ordinary language resembles a coin that we pass round among ourselves in place of something else, poetic language is like gold itself'.* [11] In poetry, language stretches to its utmost and makes itself new. It also extends its readers, being demanding of them.

Writing about Dante's *The Divine Comedy*, T S Eliot referred to a direct shock of poetic intensity. This *shock of poetry* has become a shorthand for the powerful impact of great poetic language.

Poetry exacts from the reader an attention not only to its rich subject matter, but to the gift of language itself; to meaning, tone, music and pattern; to the power of human language to move and delight.

Don Paterson suggests that *"Poetic language has two functions; to make things clear and distinct where they weren't, and to join them back up again when they were broken apart. It's a natural function of language, and the way that language, certainly, redeems itself."* [12] (By redeem, Paterson is referring to the role of language in the Edenic fall.)

In Chapters 2 and 3, I described something of the alchemic mix that characterises both leadership and poetry. An alchemic inference also can be seen in the subject matter of much poetry, including that of both William Blake and William Butler Yeats.

> *As I thought of these things, I drew aside the curtains and looked out into the darkness, and it seemed to my troubled fancy that all those little points of light filling the sky were the furnaces of innumerable divine alchemists, who labour continually, turning lead into gold, weariness into ecstasy, bodies into souls, the darkness into God; -* W. B. Yeats

Blake was also an engraver, using acid on metal to create complex pictures by stripping away its layers. A fierce and careful use of language can work in a similar way on the ground of our experience.

The Arts of Discourse

The ancient Greeks identified three different arts in any discourse: grammar (the words used), logic or dialectic (the argument or idea), and rhetoric (the use of language with persuasive effect). We balance all three in any communication. We explore logic in Chapter 17. Here, we look first at grammar, then at rhetoric.

Grammar

Poetic language can enable us to take what psychologist Jerome Bruner calls a *sideways look*. It has a *generative* grammar, that gives us a set of possible pathways to follow; to discover new linguistic intersections, byways and vistas we didn't know could exist.

Language theorists say that poetry can change our way of looking at things. For example Viktor Shklovsky [13] calls it an extensive art, suggesting that, in order to recover our feeling for the world, *"we must first of all 'shake up' things . . . We must rip things from their ordinary sequence of associations. Things must be turned over like logs in a fire."* adding, *"The poet removes the labels from things. . . . Things rebel, casting off their old names and taking on a new aspect together with their new names."*

Unlike the conventions of prose, poetry is peppered with transgressions of rules - with uncommon use of words and form, and inversions of sequence and meaning. It offers an antidote to a prosaic and utilitarian view of language that tends to dominate our time, and especially our organisational cultures. With the pre-eminence of speed, impact and the *facts* in our use of language, other qualities like depth, endurance, meaning are getting lost.

Rhetoric

It is difficult to write about the impact of leadership language without considering the ideas of rhetoric and oratory. Rhetoric is the conscious choice of words or linguistic style to persuasive effect. Nowadays we tend to see the practice of rhetoric in a bad light, associating it with spin-doctors, politicians and others deemed to be untrustworthy. Yet we use rhetoric whenever we communicate. In its broadest sense, rhetoric concerns the whole gambit of human discourse.

Rhetoric is perhaps most apparent in prepared speeches or oratory, and certainly language has a particular power when words are spoken out loud, both for our external audience, and for ourselves. Certain devices can add much to spoken language's powers of enchantment. These include the use of repetition (including liturgy and sonic repetition through rhyme), incantation (using rhythm), novelty, and metaphor or simile.

Politician Ed Miliband used rhetorical devices in his maiden speech as UK Labour party leader, including the anaphoric repetition "*Optimistic about our country. Optimistic about our world. Optimistic about the power of politics*" and an alliterative tricolon describing his predecessors Blair and Brown as "*reforming, restless and radical*".

US President Barack Obama used similar devices in his keynote speech to the 2004 Democratic convention. For example, the rhythmic sounds and repetitions in this section:

> "*That is the true genius of America, a faith... a faith in simple dreams, an insistence on small miracles; that we can tuck in our children at night and know that they are fed and clothed and safe from harm; that we can say what we think, write what we think, without hearing a sudden knock on the door; that we can have an idea and start our own business without paying a bribe; that we can participate in the political process without fear of retribution; and that our votes will be counted -- or at least, most of the time.*"

And here is Nelson Mandela's inauguration speech in 1994, ripe with repetitions, and frequent use of groups of three.

> "*We understand it still that there is no easy road to freedom.*
>
> *We know it well that none of us acting alone can achieve success.*
>
> *We must therefore act together as a united people, for national reconciliation, for nation building, for the birth of a new world.*
>
> *Let there be justice for all.*
>
> *Let there be peace for all.*
>
> *Let there be work, bread, water and salt for all.*

Let each know that for each the body, the mind and the soul have been freed to fulfill themselves.

Never, never and never again shall it be that this beautiful land will again experience the oppression of one by another and suffer the indignity of being the skunk of the world.

Let freedom reign.

The sun shall never set on so glorious a human achievement!

God bless Africa!

Thank you."

We explore linguistic devices in Chapters 10 and 11.

Dialogue

Leaders and poets need listeners. T S Eliot called poetry *one person talking to another*. Good conversation involves us in co-operating, thinking of each other's feelings and experiences, and giving each other room to talk. It is vital in the creation of an organisational culture that values thinking, learning and genuine engagement.

According to systems scientist Peter Senge, complementing systems thinking with dialogue enables people to learn as a team, creating between them a language more suited for dealing with complexity, and deep-seated issues. Such a language might be called *poetic*.

A discourse is a space where we can think, alone or with others. Clare Morgan, author of *What Poetry Brings to Business*, describes a discourse as a thinking room made of language, suggesting that its size, shape, disposition and place will influence our expression, perception and decision-making. A *stanza* - the name for a verse of poetry - is also (in Italian) a room.

Directing or Influencing

The kind of language we use changes, depending on the role we are taking in a conversation. It is not always appropriate to lead by speaking boldly. Sometimes our conversational style is made more powerful by ceding power, so that other people can be heard. The best communicator can assess the situation and match their language tool to the task.

When we need to direct the conversation, we make more declarative statements, and speak with confidence. The words we choose signal our authority. We argue comfortably with people who give opposite opinions. This is a more traditional style of leadership language, and is called for when we need to take charge of a problem, or to sound credible on a particular topic.

When we are looking to influence and engage others, to ensure that conversation takes place, we take a less central role, but can still be powerful. We elicit views and information, summarise what we have heard, check everyone's understanding of the subject. We use qualifiers (such as 'rather', 'quite', 'I think') and ask more questions. These are subtle flags that we insert to signal that we're not trying to run the conversation, but instead to keep it going so that information flows.

Dear Reader,

If I could give the strength
of all the extra-
ordinary people I know
to you:

> *a hug, a book of poems, a mural,*
> *a child on the train, a newspaper,*
> *a mic, a backpack full of books,*
> *a guitar, a pencil, a pot of soup,*
> *a concert, a protest, a prayer for peace,*

a vision of a new world...

you would cry with joy
and sadness – both –

because you would believe.

Adam Gottlieb

The Tyranny of Language

Poetic language is, by nature, complex and often ambiguous. Does this mean that it is inherently less trustworthy than prose?

German philosopher Wittgenstein argued that we are inexorably imprisoned in our language. Wittgenstein believed that the most important aspects of things can be hidden from us because they are simple and familiar, and that language is the chief culprit in this concealment. Language holds us prisoner because it brings with it a whole package of associations that we can't easily get free from. We falsely believe that words have simple and singular meanings, and these false perceptions lead us to ingrained ways of thinking that, in turn, are related to our sense that there's a way things *should* be.

If this is true, a poetic language, where meaning is consciously complex and layered - where that is its jurisdiction - may help us stay grounded.

It is in fact vital to love and distrust language. It is absolutely vital to tell truths
that catch something of the complex polyphonic music of what happens. Someone
has got to do it. It is poetry's unique task to say exactly what it means by singing it
and dancing it, by carving some crystalline pattern on the thin, cold surface of
language, thereby keeping language audible and usable. That is its straightness.
That is its legislation.

George Szirtes

How Poetry *Becomes*

Although most poetry, whether written or spoken, is *re*-cited, its genesis is largely impulsive and intuitive. It is driven by sound and rhythm. In this regard it is improvised. Like other improvised art forms, poetry provides shape, rhythm and tone, without a rigid structure.

Several linguists and philosophers write about how the emergent nature of poetry compares with the more deliberative process of writing prose. English anarchist, poet, and critic Sir Herbert Read [14] outlined poetry and prose respectively as *creative* or *constructive* expression. *"In poetry the words are born or re-born in the act of thinking. The words are, in Bergsonian* phraseology, a becoming; they develop in the mind pari passu with the development of the thought. There is no time interval between the words and the thought. The thought is the word and the word is the thought, and both the thought and the word are Poetry"*.

[* From philosopher Henri Louis Bergson, who argued that we tend to see things and states as either being or becoming.]

Poetry is making towards something, often unknown. As poet and holocaust survivor Paul Celan suggested: *"A poem, as a manifestation of language and thus essentially dialogue, can be a message in a bottle, sent out in the—not always greatly hopeful—belief that somewhere and sometime it could wash up on land, on heartland perhaps. Poems in this sense too are under way: they are making toward something."* [15]

A poetic leadership, then is strongly spontaneous and intuitive, often making toward foreign territory.

The music of what happens

According to Irish Legend's Fionn mac Cumhail, the sweetest sound in all the world is the music of what happens. Poet George Szirtes describes this 'music' as the sensation of being alive to any event, from the movement of insects to the power of a volcano; from the death of a child to the deaths of thousands.

The human mind can accommodate all this, and will try to make sense of it using a language that can categorise, connect and embellish. But, like Wittgenstein, Szirtes believes language to be untrustworthy. *"Language looks solid, but is endlessly provisional, slippery, thin and treacherous. It shines and gathers light like ice, but is fragile and likely to melt, dropping us into the inchoate world of one damn thing after another."* [16]

He makes two propositions:

1. Poets are ordinary people with a special love and distrust of language.

2. Poetry is not a pretty way of saying something straight, but the straightest way of saying something complex.

A poetic leader will pay careful attention to the music of what happens in their organisations, and will try to find straight ways to articulate what is complex.

Organisational Language

Leaders and teams who are able to draw on richer vocabulary and deeper descriptions of things, will broaden the language of their organisations and overcome the verbal monotony so common in the corporate world. To use a digital analogy, a richer organisational vocabulary can increase the bandwidth of our connections, both interpersonally and intellectually.

Such breadth lends a competitive advantage. As Karl Weick suggests in *Sensemaking In Organizations*, organisations that have access to more varied images engage in more adaptive sensemaking than organisations with limited vocabularies.

Language can also provide a window on organisational culture. We can tell a great deal from word choice, from the metaphors people use, from the tone that predominates and the stories that recur. Yet we must listen exquisitely. The true story is more likely to be discovered in the informal banter of the corridor and kitchen, than in the orchestrated performance of the board room. Organisational poetry is emergent.

Looking through a linguistic lens gives us a picture not only of a leader's objective effectiveness, but also of their subjective experience. Careful observation of a leader's choice and use of language can illuminate their thinking and decision making; it can show how the leader sees their world.

Another Country

Returning, the words were singular as stones
dripped in a still sheet of water, the clear
sense of them sinking under the surface
confusion, the prolific umming and erring.
The roads refused to add up. The school
was a coppice, the field where they'd flown
kites, a mere. There was a wild profusion
of magpies, and everyone was building
something - the prow of a church high
above the river that was the skyline.
Still, there were the vistas, the parks
with small white bridges crossing into an idea
of distance. They were just passing through.
The language returned like an underground
 stream to its source: the repeats, the three
recurrent monosyllables to describe the view.

Jane Griffiths

THE LEADER'S VOICE

Everything written is as good as it is dramatic...Sentences are not different enough to hold the attention unless they are dramatic...All that can save them is the speaking tone of voice some how entangled in the words and fastened to the page for the ear of the imagination.

Robert Frost

Finding A Voice

In this chapter we consider both the literal and figurative properties of *voice* in leadership.

Our voice is the place where language and the body meet; the vehicle through which we turn our internal thoughts into shared experience; through which we connect with others and *evoke* a response. Our words — how they are chosen, strung together and expressed — have the ability to clarify, influence, persuade and inspire.

As leaders, our voices have a significant impact on our image and long-term success. Our voice can convey integration of our inner values with our outer behaviours. Alternatively, a dissonant voice - a mismatch between tone and words, between stated values and enacted behaviours - can create a sense that something is not quite right.

In my work as a coach, I listen carefully to what people say and how they say it. Together, we explore the significance of their words and tone, and I reflect back my experience of hearing them. Their physical voice provides a window to their thoughts.

Finding A Voice is a common theme for new and developing leaders, and my clients are no exceptions. Recent clients have highlighted issues that are fundamentally to do with how they express themselves through their voice: a newly promoted manager looking for a way to embody her new role and find a different tone in her interactions with the team and her new peers; an experienced manager wanting to create the right impression in advance of (yet another set of) organisational changes - and wondering how he ensures that the clear thinking in his head is credible and convincing coming out of his mouth; a job-hunting web-designer who speaks lyrically with her watercolours, but who clams up in interviews.

These examples initially presented as relating to my clients' actual, literal voices. But using the abstract or connotative idea of '*voice*' to explore a sense of self can open up another dimension.

There was a man with tongue of wood
Who essayed to sing,
And in truth it was lamentable.
But there was one who heard
The clip-clapper of this tongue of wood
And knew what the man
Wished to sing,
And with that the singer was content.

Stephen Crane

The concept of voice is closely related to our sense of identity. In choosing the voice we use, for example as leaders, we are saying something about the kind of person we want to be seen as. A successful leader needs to find out who they really are - their beliefs and values and passions - and how to express this in a way which energises people rather than dominates them.

Authentic leadership is the art of mastering and authoring both ourself and our message; of finding and mastering our unique voice - one that is unmistakable from anyone else. If our voice doesn't reflect the kind of person we truly are, however much we might admire those we would model ourselves on, we will struggle to make that noise.

Poets make conscious choices about the voice in which they write. Whilst it may change in tone from one work to another, many poets have a characteristic style. Although, like the poet, we will adapt and modify our words and tone to fit the audience or situation, our unique leadership voice must remain recognisable. We must not lose ourselves in order to fit in. If a leader is to create trust and confidence, they must sound true; they must act and speak consistently.

How Saint Christina sang

"Then she stopped spinning and sang.
No-one could imitate the sounds that came from deep in her chest
nor make sense of the syllables; no breath came from out of her nose or mouth,
but it was like angels singing" - Thomas de Chantimpre

think of it like a Mongolian trance-chant
sung on the bottomless in-breath
like a journey along the silk road
being rolled back past the dust-heaps
and broken walls of frontier towns, back
past the one remaining window made
of a slice of lapis lazuli and the still wind-chimes
back into the rib-cage, the swaddle, the chrysalis
or find in your mind an Inuit song
sung by one by two sister-twins
like the ice-night and the eery not-sun lights
hologramming on the sky's retina
breathing down each other's wind-pipes
the in-out of the ice-sheet across the eyelids
the sound-harpoon in the blank ice-pool
see, she does not cloud the mirror

Jane Draycott and Lesley Saunders in *Christina the Astonishing*

Resonance

A compelling voice is sometimes referred to as *resonating*, meaning that it has a certain quality of sound that is deep, full, and reverberating. Resonance also relates to the impact of our words; the ability to *evoke* or suggest images, memories, and emotions; to bring dry arguments to life. Great leaders exude resonance - a passion for their mission - which can be contagious. It can elicit from their audience a resounding 'yes!'

Our stories, explanations and reasoned arguments can be resonant or dissonant. A resonant voice will integrate inner values with outer behaviours; whereas a dissonant voice just doesn't sound right. So, too, a favourite poem will resonate with us, and can trigger strong responses.

Resonance can also refer to being in tune, for example with the organisational mood. Resonant leaders pick up the current mood; they know when to be collaborative and when to be visionary; when to listen and when to command.

Resonant communication creates rapport, and may include elements of mirroring. Strengthening rapport improves our communication links. The content of our messages will be more easily heard if the connection is strong. In contrast, our communication channels and sense of connection can be easily damaged by tone, especially by distance, cynicism and negativity.

The Inner Voice

As well as the outer voices we express, we have inner voices too, although we may be less aware of them. Some of these voices are not really ours. They are the nagging voices of fear, regret or embarrassment; the voice of a teacher, parent or boss who shamed us; the envious voices of others who ask "who do you think you are?". Some call these voices Gremlins. As a coach and facilitator, I am often helping a client or participant to challenge these voices.

We also have our own, genuine, inner voice. The one that reflects the meaning we place on our experiences and the lessons we have learned. The one that has guiding wisdom to offer. It might be more subtle and less heard than the one we usually employ in public, especially in the workplace. It often gets ignored and may be forced to get our attention in different ways - through a gut feeling, a sense of separation or longing, or the physical ramifications of stress. We usually do well to listen to it.

As leaders, bringing out more of this inner voice can engage people in deeply held values and beliefs, and in the future we are striving to create. In my own experience, this inner voice is more lyrical, questioning and open-minded. I think it is poetic.

Overhearing, and The Sweet Territory of Silence

A coaching relationship is one way of creating a space in which a client can *overhear* herself. Overhearing is different to hearing. When we overhear something we catch its essence and overall sense rather than its detail, like seeing an object out of the corner of our eye. It is a snatched moment; a glimpsed insight of something in our peripheral vision; something we might easily have missed in our busyness or business; something that we may not spot if we are striving to hear it. We need to approach it with stealth.

Writers such as John Stuart Mill and Robert Frost have described poetry and poetic tone as *overheard*. Often we are not so much overhearing the poet as we are catching something of our own voice in their words; like glimpsing ourselves in a mirror, rather than gazing full-on. Reading great works, including poetry, is a powerful way to learn important truths about ourselves without any stifling self-consciousness.

One reason we fail to hear what is truly important, is that our lives are full of noise. Sometimes we ourselves are the main culprits, engaging in inner chatter and endless activity as if we don't know how to stop; as if we are afraid of what we might notice if we did.

The Quiet World

> *In an effort to get people to look*
> *into each other's eyes more,*
> *and also to appease the mutes,*
> *the government has decided*
> *to allot each person exactly one hundred*

and sixty-seven words, per day.
When the phone rings, I put it to my ear
without saying hello. In the restaurant
I point at chicken noodle soup.
I am adjusting well to the new way.
Late at night, I call my long distance lover,
proudly say I only used fifty-nine today.
I saved the rest for you.
When she doesn't respond,
I know she's used up all her words,
so I slowly whisper I love you
thirty-two and a third times.
After that, we just sit on the line
and listen to each other breathe.

Jeffrey McDaniel

Silence can be frightening and unpredictable. It can feel like being alone. But there is comfort in it too as Gabrielle Roth suggests in *Maps to Ecstasy:* "*In many shamanic societies, if you came to a medicine person complaining of being disheartened, dispirited, or depressed, they would ask one of four questions. When did you stop dancing? When did you stop singing? When did you stop being enchanted by stories? When did you stop finding comfort in the sweet territory of silence?*". [17]

Listening Deep

As Jean Cocteau said, "*The poet doesn't invent. He listens.*" Such a poet cannot write without silence and stillness; without the inner solitude that allows a deep and intent listening to her feelings. Silence is of course necessary if, as leaders, we wish to have a voice that listens. So often, even when we are silent, we are not really listening; we are just waiting to speak.

Perhaps as leaders we could all make more space for this kind of silence in our lives. Maybe we would hear something really important. Perhaps we would create a place where others are more able to hear themselves too.

"We can make our minds so like still water that beings gather about us, that they may see their own images, and so live for a moment with a clearer, perhaps even a fiercer life, because of our quiet." - W.B. Yeats

For the busy leader, poetry might be a bit of a Trojan horse - but one truly full of gifts - a way with words that can get past our doubts and defences, and help us to hear or see what is important. Poetry uses a number of linguistic devices and tricks that can jolt our brains into a different awareness.

Tone of Voice

The idea of tone has relevance in poetry, leadership and in organisations as a whole. When we talk about someone's 'tone of voice' we are referring to the many ways in which a voice may enrich or modify the meanings of spoken words, and create a certain mood or atmosphere.

Tone refers to the musical aspects of voice - pitch, volume, pace, and emphasis - that we respond instinctively to. Human speech has a huge variety of tones and these, as much as the actual words spoken, will spark a particular emotional response and support or detract from the speaker's reasoning.

There are some people whose vocal tone has a positive effect on others; who have a warm and welcoming voice quality; the kind of person who can make the most boring training manual sound interesting. Other people's vocal tone can be off-putting, whether uncertain, cold, whiney or bullish.

Some poets reading their own work bring the words to life off the page. Dylan Thomas, Kathleen Jamie, Ted Hughes and Gwendolyn Brooks are among my personal favourites.

The Pool Players. Seven at The Golden Shovel

We real cool. We
Left school. We

Lurk late. We
Strike straight. We

Sing sin. We
Thin gin. We

Jazz June. We
Die soon.

Gwendolyn Brooks

Others, whether through nerves or artistry - a mimicry of other poets' readings perhaps? - may lapse into a 'poetry voice' that can be soporific at best and irritating at worst.

Our tone is a vital component of our credibility as leaders, and the audience's ears are as important as their eyes in judging our leadership abilities. Successful leaders use a combination of charm and authority in their vocal tone and vocabulary to influence and motivate their audiences. Vocal tone conveys our overall attitude; the purpose or feeling we wish to convey. A strong, clear, confident voice commands authority. It suggests that we are familiar with success, and comfortable with ourselves and others. It says 'follow me'. Balanced with an appropriate seasoning of humility and humour, of pathos and surprise, our vocal tone can help to build a followership.

Such a balance is not easy to achieve; there is no simple, all-encompassing recipe. We can learn vocal technique, but effective expression is as much about developing a strong sense of self. One approach that may help is to think poetically about our voices.

Pitch and Volume

We make instinctive judgements of others based upon the voice pitch of the speaker. People with deeper voices are perceived as having more authority and greater confidence, whilst a high pitched or shrill voice tends to have a negative effect and can be irritating. This is believed to be partly cultural throw back, to a time where status was based largely on physical power and strength.

Vocal volume is important too - it is a key way in which we convey energy and spirit to our audience, whether a conference room of a thousand, a team meeting of ten or a crucial one-to-one encounter.

Being heard as a leader is not only about the volume of our words, but about our ability to speak difficult truths and to stand up there when the wave hits the rock. Often our actions, body language and mood speak louder than our words. Our energy and presence will set the tone for the organisation. At times, too, we will need to have a quieter voice - one that listens and allows others to bloom; to take centre stage. We need a lightness of touch, like a conductor holding their baton.

In poetry, pitch and volume are most apparent when spoken aloud, the reader making conscious choices about their style of oration. The style of spoken word, slam or performance poetry, for example, is generally louder and more direct than that of more lyrical poetic genres. A poet may use a deeper pitch in a celebratory or rallying piece, and a higher, lighter note in a poem that is inquisitive or intimate. Poets also use linguistic devices to signal aspects of poetic tone - which may include volume and pitch - in their work on the page.

Pace making

One simple change that most of us could make if we wish to communicate better, is to slow down. If we speak more slowly, it has a number of positive effects on our communication.

Firstly, it gives the person listening enough time to digest the message. This means not just hearing it with their ears, but understanding it with their mind. It takes effort and time to focus the mind on meaning and to make it clear and distinct. It is important to give enough time for our message to "sink in" before delivering the next one.

Secondly, people who speak slightly slower are perceived by the listener to be deeper and more thoughtful, compared with faster speakers who are perceived to be lightweight and confusing. When we slow down, it suggests that we are thinking before we speak; that we are weighing up the facts and giving careful consideration to our response. And if we take it slowly, we will have more time to select the right words to express our meaning exactly.

As with other elements of tone, there are times when we need to set the pace within a conversation or an organisation, and times when we need to follow. It is useful to think about organisational changes that would enable us all to slow down more.

Poetry is full of characteristics and devices that encourage us to slow down as we read (or write) it.

Emphasis

The best communicators have a dynamism in the way they use their voice. Varying our vocal tone injects life and energy into our message, and enables us to emphasise key words and ideas. In contrast, people find it hard to focus on content spoken in a monotone or lifeless voice. Emotions in particular - such as passion, urgency or concern - are conveyed by changes in the tone of our voice.

Vocal modulation is also important in providing contrast - light and shade. If all of our communication is uniformly bright, nothing stands out. We will need to vary different aspects of our voice - pitch, volume, pace and stress - in order to have impact. The linguistic term for this is prosody. We will explore aspects of prosody in poetry in later chapters

Extract from *The Map*

Land lies in water; it is shadowed green.
Shadows, or are they shallows, at its edges
showing the line of long sea-weeded ledges
where weeds hang to the simple blue from green.
Or does the land lean down to lift the sea from under,
drawing it unperturbed around itself?

Elizabeth Bishop

The Poetic Voice and the Audience

Like great leaders, every poet is a dramatist. The poet chooses a voice or voices for her particular poem and imagines some kind of audience for the voices.

In many poems the poet speaks in his own voice, apparently to himself or to no one in particular, in a tone that we believe reflects their inner state (as we see in much of Walt Whitman's poetry, such as *Song of Myself*).

In a dramatic monologue, such as *Soliloquy of the Spanish Cloister* by Robert Browning, the poet may write in the voice of one person speaking to another. We may hear undertones of the creator's own outlook as expressed through the words of his protagonist.

This technique is sometimes extended to a dialogue, with two voices in a poem arguing different positions, as in *The Way* by Edwin Muir. Often the voices in such a poem completely absorb us and we are not aware of the author's speaking at all. In this way the poet can pre-empt our anxieties and, in the next breath, reply to them. This is a useful and common approach in leadership rhetoric.

In poems of direct address, such as *The Sun Rising by* John Donne, the poet speaks to another individual or some personified object or abstraction. This is their first audience. But the poet will also be aware of the eavesdroppers - the readers or listeners - whose interests she hopes to excite.

Similarly, a leader's audience is always wider than the individual or group currently being addressed - their words and actions are overheard, repeated, re-interpreted. So as leaders we must write not just the rhetorical set pieces of the board room and the news letter, but the mood music and corridor conversations, ripe with eavesdropped and implied messages.

Passivity

One voice we tend to hear a lot in the workplace is the *passive*. In the passive voice, the noun or noun phrase that would be the object of an active sentence (such as Brutus stabbed *Caesar*) appears as the subject of a sentence (e.g. *Caesar* was stabbed by Brutus). The passive voice tends to sound more evasive than its active equivalent.

The passive voice is sometimes used to distance the speaker from their actions. For example, operator of the USA's biggest ever fraud scheme, Bernard Madoff, speaking at his trial in 2009 said: "*When I began the Ponzi scheme, I believed **it would end** shortly, and I would be able to extricate myself, and my clients, from the scheme.*" and "*To the best of my recollection, **my fraud began** in the early nineteen-nineties.*"

The tendency to distance ourselves from uncomfortable truths results from cognitive dissonance; from our inability to accept that we have done wrong. This phenomenon is explored in Tavris and Aronson's book *Mistakes Were Made (But Not by Me)*. The iconic phrase '*Mistakes Were Made*' is famed for its use by pundits and politicians to distance themselves from wrongdoing. Examples include White House Press Secretary Ron Ziegler, speaking about the Watergate affair, and U.S. President Ronald Reagan, while discussing what came to be known as the arms-for-hostages scandal within the Iran-Contra affair.

Points of View

The poet's point-of-view concentrates on the vantage point of the speaker, or "teller" of the poem.

Using the first person, or *I*, the speaker is a character in the poem and tells it from his or her perspective. This approach lends immediacy and the audience's sympathy is likely to be more intense. However, some argue that in the first person, the poet can only authentically write what she personally knows or sees.

> *I know I am solid and sound,*
> *To me the converging objects of the universe perpetually flow,*
> *All are written to me, and I must get what their writing means.*

Walt Whitman, *Song of Myself, 20*

Writing using the second person, "Dear Reader", a poet will address *you*, the reader, (or an imagined listener) directly as if you are reading it at the same time I am writing it. A second person voice can give writing intimacy and draw you in. Although it can sound instructional if used throughout a piece of prose, it is more achievable in poetry, as if the poet is catching your eye and asking you to share in a moment with them.

> *Do not weep, maiden, for war is kind.*

Stephen Crane, *War Is Kind*

Most poetry is written in the third person, about *him/her/them*. In the third person limited, the speaker is not part of the story. They will tell us about all the characters, but will only know about the feelings and viewpoints of one character.

> *I met a traveler from an antique land.*

Shelley, *Ozymandias*

In the third person omniscient: the speaker is again not part of the story, but, as God-like narrator, he is able to "know" and describe what all characters are thinking. This allows the writer to describe how he or she sees a scene as if watching a movie. Although the reader may feel alienated from the main character as we don't know how they feel, this can be achieved using 'third person intimate' narration in which an omniscient narrator is also able to focus on one character's intimate thoughts and feelings.

from *The Seven Of Pentacles*

Under a sky the color of pea soup
she is looking at her work growing away there
actively, thickly like grapevines or pole beans
as things grow in the real world, slowly enough.

Marge Piercy

In leadership conversations we need to take care which point of view to use. Typically we might be advised to avoid the use of "I". This relates in part to the idea of humility and servant leadership. However, there are times when it is important to share our personal view, or to take individual responsibility for action. "I" is vital here.

"We" should be a frequent Point of View for the inclusive leader, when articulating a shared experience or challenge. However, its overuse can create confusion about who needs to do what.

When using the third person in leadership conversations, to refer to other employees, customers or shareholders, for example, we need to avoid de-personalisation and over-generalisation. A skilled leader will often use the third person intimate to create a vivid picture of what they believe another person - a customer, shareholder or competitor for example - wants or believes. This often includes a storytelling perspective.

In this book I use a blend of second person - you - when focusing on you as a reader, first person plural - we - when talking about our shared experience as leaders, and third person (intimate) - he/she - when talking about how poets write. Whilst I see myself as both a leader and a poet, our shared experience is in leadership, and I am assuming that, in the main, you, the reader, currently have a third person point of view regarding poets.

Perspective

To be effective a leader must move back and forth between the dance floor and balcony. They can't effect action up on the balcony; to have impact, they must be on the dance floor. But their perspective is clearest and widest from the balcony. To make an assessment of the overall situation, they must disengage from the moment and step back. This is like moving away from the first person singular point of view; taking the 'I' - and the ego - out of leading.

According to William Stafford: "*In its essence, poetry, like other sustained human endeavors, is done best in a condition of humility and welcoming of what comes. The exploration of what the materials of life can yield to us, and the discovery of what is implicit in human experience, will work best for one who is turned outward, with trust, with courage, and with a ready yielding to what time brings into view. This practice can be the opposite of egotistical.*" [18]

Like any publicly exercised skill, both leadership and the writing of poetry can easily be egotistical manoeuvres: it takes conscious effort to approach our metier with fluency and grace.

> *not there, not yet*
>   *the gull still*
> *becoming the cloud that chases the boy,*
> *or the boy puts himself into the water*
> *like moose or dark elk tasting lichen.*
> *no, not yet: if you never arrive,*

you never have to choose between trails,
one going up past the waterfall's steam,
another idling in the heat, stirred
by the strokes of gnats' wings—
the story doesn't have to end; the telling
braids words into watercress, the cry of the rabbit,
caught in the lynx' jaws, rings out
over the reeds, echoes never receding.

Art Durkee

Tense - Past, Present and Future

Leaders must balance their attention, and the focus they create for others, between events in the past, present and future.

In literature, past tense gives us confidence that the narrator has all the facts, and can reflect on their meaning for us. It can come across as dogmatic, taking away the reader's ability to interpret for themselves. Reflecting on the past, both to understand an organisation's roots and to learn from mistakes, is a key part of a leader's sensemaking role. Too much dwelling in those places, however, can keep an organisation stuck in its ways, or lead to a blaming culture.

The present tense offers a greater sense of immediacy as we experience events alongside with the teller. The facts may be more slippery. In literature, this can add an effective tension to the text.

In organisations, use of the present tense - focusing on the here and now - creates relevance for people and engages them more. Encouraging clients to '*be here, now*' - to practice being in the moment and suspend any ruminations on the past and anxieties about the future - is an important component in the coaching and workshops offered at *Different Development*.

Although stories are rarely written in the future tense, some poetry is written as a musing on the shape of things to come. As leaders we often think and talk about the future, creating a vision and building ownership.

Effective leaders also use presupposition to great effect, speaking with an assumption that plans will come to fruition. This linguistic approach is powerful in coaching conversations. Shakespeare used it to great effect in the famous Saint Crispin's Day Speech from Henry V.

> *And gentlemen in England now a-bed*
> *Shall think themselves accursed they were not here,*
> *And hold their manhoods cheap whiles any speaks*
> *That fought with us upon Saint Crispin's day.*

As leaders, we need to be able to link past, present and future in a seamless story: to make sense of events of the past and articulate how they impact on the present; to describe how actions in the present will lead to a desired (or undesired future), or in reverse, how the future we wish for requires us to act in certain ways today.

Our focus may frequently rest on past and future, and is often drawn, rightly, to outside drivers, including customer perspectives, shareholder demands and external reporting systems. In order to create immediate relevance for the people we lead, we may need to find new ways to keep our voices in the present.

9

A VOCATION:

LETTING YOUR LIFE SPEAK

The real change takes place within our souls; the real change takes place when the unfolding of our souls reflects in some deep, mysterious way the unfolding of the universe. Then it is – when an individual person dares to live within his or her truth – that the world is changed, forever.

Vaclav Havel

Choosing a Vocation

In this chapter, we explore what it means to develop a sense of ourselves as leaders with integrity, originality and authenticity. We have already looked at the importance of choosing a voice to lead with. Here we consider how the very fact of being a leader, and the kind of leader we are, is evocative; a way of voicing our selves.

The word vocation comes from the same root as voice. Parker Palmer builds on this link in his book *Let Your Life Speak*, suggesting that before we can tell our life what we want to do with it, we must listen to our life telling us who we are. Finding our vocation, our authentic voice, is partly about finding and being ourself, the person we're created to be. Strong leaders have an identity separate to that of the company; they are clear about their individual persona, their unique life purpose.

> Extract from *Juggling in Church*,
>
> *Though he spoke plainly in oak, any wood would do him,*
> *bloodwood or blue gum too if they'd had Cornish roots.*
> *If words were trees, he'd have worked those for meanings,*
> *making sense of their gulunggal-twisting grain.*
> *Some men are like that.*
>
> Don Barnard

How do we come to leadership - or ultimately, to decide that this form of leading (this sector, organisation or chair person) is not for us? For some, such clarity exists from an early age. For others it is unearthed, slowly, and often through adversity, or simply through many wrong turns taken before we find the right path. Sometimes the only way to find our path is to stop looking.

One route to vocation is simply to find out what we are uniquely good at, and then to do it relentlessly until we find its purpose; the intersection between our unique talent and the market. This takes passion, commitment and resilience.

The Riddle of Here

We're looking. For something so simple.

*So simple, that we can't hold it in
our hands. Or in our heads.*

*So we look to him. To her.
To them. To there.*

*We look to everywhere but here.
To when. To then. But not to now.*

It's hidden just beyond our cleverness.

So we presume it's out there.

But perhaps it's in here.

Nic Askew

Perhaps the toughest test for the leader today is not one of knowledge and strategies but of identity and purpose. We are seeking meaning - a way of belonging in the world. Doing good work is one of the ultimate ways to live a good life; to make our mark.

Sometimes it helps to say who we are out loud, to ourselves or to others. The words "*I am a writer*" or "*I am a leader*" can be powerful; far more so than "*I write a little*" or "*In my job I guide others*". Our felt reaction to hearing the words out loud can be very telling. We may be giving voice to our true selves, and letting our lives speak. Indeed, authentic leaders are comfortable with the sound of their own voice; they are connected to their message and to its vehicle.

Sometimes leadership, in its broad sense, is simply speaking up or making our presence known because we have no choice - we can no longer stay silent or hidden - expressing our selves as Vaclav Havel, Gandhi and Rosa Parks all did.

Becoming Who We Are

Poetry celebrates idiosyncrasy; the colour and texture of human life that bring joy and beauty as well as presenting some of our greatest challenges. Many feel it has a special role in helping us to find our identity - our particular way of being in and belonging to the world - and in strengthening our belief in the internal images by which we make sense of the complicated and sometimes chaotic world we live in.

We each have a unique 'signature' - spoken in our gestures, and pauses, infused in our choice of words and the sounds of our voice. It may be a product of the culture or landscape we were raised in, of rootlessness, or of life events - affirming or challenging. Being true to this aspect of our voice can keep us grounded.

Poets show us this essential signature in their writing: Seamus Heaney's boggy landscapes and vowel meadows, Walt Whitman's rhythm-filled Manhattan pavements; Angela Readman's surreal imagery; Jo Shapcott's diamond-hard observations.

Hairless

Can the bald lie? The nature of the skin says not:
it's newborn-pale, erection-tender stuff,
every thought visible,—pure knowledge,
mind in action—shining through the skull.
I saw a woman, hairless absolute, cleaning.
She mopped the green floor, dusted bookshelves,
all cloth and concentration, Queen of the moon.

You can tell, with the bald, that the air
speaks to them differently, touches their heads
with exquisite expression. As she danced
her laundry dance with the motes, everything
she ever knew skittered under her scalp.
It was clear just from the texture of her head,
she was about to raise her arms to the sky;
I covered my ears as she prepared to sing, to roar.

Jo Shapcott

Integrity

Leadership, like writing, can be lonely place. Our focus is on others - our audience. We are required to support people, but may not be able to seek solace from others at work. We need to be able to sustain ourselves. We need to develop resilience and find ways to remind ourselves of our place in the world.

A sense of integrity is not about how others see us. It is something felt by the individual, also described as being undivided or undefended.

Theories of defendedness suggest that the messages we receive from an early age (from parents, teachers, and society) can lead us to believe that it is not safe to be out in the world as our true selves. As a result, we can grow into a life where our inner selves are disconnected from our outer selves, and where we feel a need to defend ourselves. One strategy of defended leadership is to build separate front and back stages, allowing us to reveal or conceal aspects of our self according to how threatening we perceive our audience to be. However, hiding the truth from our detractors in order to avoid conflict can leave us with a sense of discord - of being out of integrity.

In contrast, in a leader with a high degree of integrity, these inner and outer selves are one - integrated. Such leaders share their inner truth outwardly, and are known for who they truly are at their core. They have the courage to stand in the face of criticism; to engage in conflict for the sake of what they believe in. They don't try to please everyone.

In great poetry too there is a sense of disclosure; of integrity and fit.

Becoming a Leader

We saw in Chapter 7 how poetry is *a becoming*; is not static, but *making towards*. Poetry can be a vehicle to work ideas out; a means of shaping the shaper. Many authors describe the creative process as being a way to write themselves into (or out of) something. For example, David Grossman describes the process of writing his book *Falling Out Of Time*, following the death of his son, as a way of writing himself back to life saying "*I felt if I was unfortunate enough to be sent to this place of bereavement, at least I'll try to map it.*" [19]

Leadership of our selves is a creative process too. As self-authors we imagine and write ourselves into presence; we *become what we write*. That is our true *authority* - the narrative process though which an authentic self emerges. In every leadership act - in each choice we make - we are creating a persona that is recognised not only by others, but - most importantly - by ourselves.

I imagine that very few children want to be 'a leader' when they grow up, and people are often surprised to find themselves in a leadership role. For professional groups (such as doctors or social workers), this often means taking on a leadership position amongst peers and ex-colleagues, and can be especially challenging. Having a clear leadership identity - being able to articulate why people should follow you - is important. After all, if you don't believe in your vocation as a leader, why should anyone else?

We looked in Chapter 3 at the unspoken contract that exists between poet and reader: the willing response or followership. A similar pattern of expectation and attribution is at play in organisational contexts between the leaders and the led. A leader is a leader because of their position and role; because they say (or someone else says) that they are.

Leaders may be given a role, or may acquire that status through their actions and persona. Either way there are unwritten as well as written contracts that set out certain expectations, both of leaders and of followers. An effective leader will cultivate a willing followership and act in a way that results in their attribution with leadership qualities. Followers will always read deeply into any leadership communication, so leaders need to be care-full with their messages.

Authentic Leadership

The concept of authentic leadership has been detailed by writers such as Avolio and Gardner, and W G George. According to George, authentic leaders focus on purpose, meaning and values; they lead with heart and through connected relationships; they demonstrate discipline and self-development.

Truly authentic leaders are anchored by a deep sense of self. This is where they stand.

> *"Give me the place to stand, and I shall move the world."* - Archimedes

Although true authenticity - behaving *in accordance with the true self* - does not involve us considering the perception of others, it is seen and judged in relationship with others. Indeed, authenticity is one of the key characteristics that followers attribute to leaders they admire. Authentic leadership depends on a leader's relations with others, because all leadership is relational at its core. Similarly, whilst poetry is not usually written for the audience, all poetry needs a reader.

There is a strong link between authenticity and what psychologists call self-actualisation. Self-actualised people are in tune with their basic nature and accurately see themselves and their lives. They feel good in their skin. Because they are uninhibited by the expectations of others, they can make sounder choices. Of course authentic leaders are not immune from bias. However they are more inclined to consider numerous perspectives in order to assess information in a balanced way. In this way they help to promote transparent relationships and decision-making, and to build trust and commitment.

Leadership is authenticity, not style. Authentic leaders are originals. Much of the literature on leadership development contains lists of the leadership characteristics we are supposed to adopt, and extols the virtues of particular leaders we are recommended to emulate. This is the antithesis of authenticity. It is about developing a persona or an image of a leader: a high ego, style-over-character, hero-celebrity leader. The prospective leader who attempts to adopt a list of defined leadership traits is destined to fail.

In the Margins

where I've always lived:
salt marsh, at the edge
of word and image.

Liminal, ambivalent,
in the more acceptable
domains of the outlawed,
where normal is conjured,
clothed in motley.

Between hang of sky and seep of mud,
hedgerow and furrow, thicket
and drainpipe, town and nightgown
caught by cloud drift and shadow,
tumble of rock and snicket.

This cleft is my habitat, its tilt
of tree, echo of wing-flap
woodpigeon, kestrel
sailing the space of its negative
one slope to the other; their grace.

Rachael Clyne

We cannot imitate other people's leadership. We can't be another Steve Jobs or Anita Roddick by mimicry, because what successful leaders have in common is not a particular style, but the generic traits of substance and integrity. We must learn to be our own kind of leaders.

Authentic leaders can also help to foster the development of authenticity in others. In sharing ourselves fully at work, and showing that we value difference, we can help others to find their unique voice. This is a far cry from the kind of charismatic leadership that encourages carbon-copy followers. In turn, the ability of people around us to act authentically will contribute to a sense of well-being and to sustainable performance, building human, social and psychological capital.

Helping others to grow requires us to put our egos aside. Leadership is responsibility and a key aspect of that responsibility is to empower and develop others. Perhaps, above all, leadership and work are about love?

Work is love made visible - Kahlil Gibran

10

SOUNDING IT OUT:
RHYME & RESONANCE

It's tone I'm in love with; that's what poetry is, tone.

Robert Frost

Sound Signatures

More than in any other medium, poetry uses sound to convey meaning. A poet is sensitive to the sounds words make and guides her audience to meaning using technique as well as content. Through the simple yet demanding act of combining consonants and vowels in certain ways, a poet can communicate emotions that are distinct from the words' denotations and connotations.

Sonic or 'phonemic' devices such as repetition, assonance, mimesis and rhythm enable the poet to overlay and stress certain sounds, with powerful and sometimes intoxicating effect. These aspects of poetic voice, alongside the images and events in the poem, work to create mood and enhance emotion; to make music from words.

A poet can create a kind of facsimile of oral performance, using marks on the page as sound clues that signal how the reader might 'hear' the poem, in their audile imagination, and help to reproduce the vocal tone, gesture, and stance of her oration. As Robert Frost wrote: "*The visual images thrown up by a poem are important, but it is more important still to choose and arrange words in a sequence so as to virtually control the intonations and pauses of the reader's voice.*" [20]

The key elements of the sound signature of a poem - known as *prosody* - are *rhythm*, *metre* and *intonation*. Sound effects are achieved in various ways in different genres of poetry, often responding to the characteristics of the language in which the poet writes. Classical formal English poetry typically uses an iambic metre, and either blank (unrhymed) verse or end rhymes to create its sound signature.

V. The Soldier

If I should die, think only this of me:
  That there's some corner of a foreign field
That is for ever England. There shall be
  In that rich earth a richer dust concealed;
A dust whom England bore, shaped, made aware,

Gave, once, her flowers to love, her ways to roam,
A body of England's, breathing English air,
  Washed by the rivers, blest by suns of home.

And think, this heart, all evil shed away,
 A pulse in the eternal mind, no less
  Gives somewhere back the thoughts by England given;
Her sights and sounds; dreams happy as her day;
 And laughter, learnt of friends; and gentleness,
  In hearts at peace, under an English heaven.

Rupert Brooks

Other poetic traditions use alternatives means of achieving euphony, for example the dense regulation of chinese lüshi poetry, or the unrhymed alliterative lines of epic Saxon poetry such as Beowulf.

The Home Key

No matter how complexity, tension and dissonance give life to an organisation, we need there to be some point of reference - a destination - to make sense of the rich variation. This is like the *home key* in a piece of music, or the pervading *tone* in a poem, and provides a coherent structure or overall vision. As leaders we must be alert to the connotative 'tone' we are creating within our organisations.

As we saw in Chapter 8, *vocal* tone is a key determinant of leadership success. In poetry there are many ways to set the tone, and these may have their equivalents in leadership. In this chapter we explore some of the phonemic components with which poetry enlivens language, and consider their role in leadership.

Balancing Sound & Sense

The sound of the poem should embody its symbols, it should inspire - breathe life into - the poem's meaning. A poet will try to match sound and sense - making the one support the other - to create a coherent whole. Yet poetry is a constant tension between music and meaning.

The competing schemes of metre and syntax make for some of this tension; the overall song of the rhythm, with the sound and meaning of individual words. It is also a tension between mystery and clarity; impression and expression; what is said and the *more* than what is said.

A poet must decide whether sound should be a secondary, supporting element, serving the sense of the piece, or whether it can play a dominant role, and if so, when? Overdoing the sound effects may irritate or amuse the audience. Most poets will try to infuse phonemic techniques naturally into their poems in ways that do not bring undue attention to them. In making these choices, the poet is finding a balance between the content of their message, and the vehicle or medium by which it is transmitted.

As leaders, we make similar choices when we focus our attention on the details of a task at hand, or on the relationships needed to deliver this and future tasks. Neither alone can succeed. In many busy working environments, task focus is given priority, sometimes at the expense of relationship and engagement. Whilst task focus may be efficient in the short term, a focus on relationships will strengthen rapport and build commitment and resilience. The poetic leader manages this balance with care.

Extract from *Song of Myself* by Walt Whitman

I hear the sound I love, the sound of the human voice,
I hear all sounds running together, combined, fused or following,
Sounds of the city and sounds out of the city, sounds of the day and night,
Talkative young ones to those that like them, the loud laugh of work-
people at their meals,

Tone and Style

A poem's tone is its overall mood or pervading atmosphere; the attitude towards the subject that its style implies; its *emotional colouring*. A poet uses tone to influence the readers' expectations and response. Dylan Thomas' tone is fierce and imperative in his famous villanelle about death, *Do Not Go Gentle Into That Good Night*.

American poet laureate Robert Frost believed it was voice tone or the *'sound of sense'* which conveyed art in poetry, suggesting that poetry should be about things we recognise, things common in experience, but delightful in the uncommon way a thing is said. When Frost spoke and wrote about tone, he meant the kind of *eavesdropped* vocal sound that comes through a closed door when people are speaking - the kind that gives us a clear sense of what is going on even though we can't hear the words exactly.

Likewise, people should be able to understand what is going on in an organisation (or a leader's mind) from the overheard tones in an organisations's conversational register. As they will inevitably hear something, it is important that what they hear is what we as leaders would want them to hear. We need to be deliberate. The tone of ongoing practices, habits and processes; the attitude implied by the things we pay attention to; the symbolism of our daily decisions and choices - these may be more pervasive in setting the tone than formal communications and Board reports. Tone needs to be consistent and congruent, supporting the sense of what we are trying to say.

Tone in poetry shows itself most obviously in diction - in sounds and words - but it is also infused in the images, cadences, and other events of a poem. So too in organisations, our non verbal signals and symbols will be carefully read and will be taken to signify the organisation's culture and values; the leaders' attitudes. We must choose symbolic acts and activities that support our spoken messages, and have the desired emotional impact. One way to remind ourselves of this, is to think *poetically* - or *tonally* - about our actions.

Over time, poetry readers learn to hear intonation with their mind's ear, and to recognise the clues to tone that a poet has scattered through the poem. Tone isn't usually heard in one specific place of a poem - it pervades the whole piece; its general attitude. Tone can also shift through a poem and this is often part of what is most intriguing and enjoyable about it.

Examples of tone in poetry, some appearing in this book, include:

* confessional: *Listen! I will be honest with you* (*Song of the Open Road*, Walt Whitman)

* ironic: *Do not weep, maiden, for war is kind.* (*War Is Kind*, Stephen Crane,).

* surreal: *World is crazier and more of it than we think / Incorrigibly plural.* (*Snow*, Louis MacNeice)

* ominous: *the sea blinks and rolls / like a worried eyeball* (*Rowing*, Anne Sexton)

* delicate: *Like any other day, the early sun slips / slantwise through the criss-cross railway bridge.* (*Incident*, Jane Griffiths)

* intimate: *What scent of old wood hovers, what softened / sound from outside fills the air?* (*You Reading This, Be Ready*, William Stafford)

* reverent: *To see a world in a grain of sand, / And a heaven in a wild flower,* (*Augeries of Innocence* - William Blake)

* angry: *If you could hear, at every jolt, the blood / Come gargling from the froth-corrupted lungs,* (*Dulce Et Decorum Est,* Wilfred Owen)

* drowsy: *The moan of doves in immemorial elms/ And murmuring of innumerable bees.* (from *Come Down, O Maid* by Lord Alfred Tennyson)

There are certain tones in poetry that tend to attract or frustrate us. We don't like poems to be smug, elusive or too clever. Neither do we appreciate these attitudes in our leaders.

Say That Again!

Poets often repeat themselves. Repetition of same or similar words, sounds, symbols, even lines, helps to create a sense of congruence and flow; a thread that we can follow through the labyrinth of a poem.

Betweenland X

Just after sunset, and the tide
high, almost white, dull-
lambent like nothing the sky

holds or could lend it. Each
shore, this and that shore,
black, a particular

blackness pinned in place
by each house- or street-lamp.
Done with. As if land

was night, and us its night-thoughts
and the river was the draining down
of daylight, westwards and out

of the world, so how could you not
(your gaze at least) feel drawn
and want, half want, to follow?

Philip Gross

Repetition can also help to give a sense of completeness or inevitability to a poem, especially if the poem's ending somehow echoes its beginning; we are invited to circle back and make new links, as seen in Alice Oswald's poem *Wedding*.

Wedding

From time to time our love is like a sail
and when the sail begins to alternate
from tack to tack, it's like a swallowtail
and when the swallow flies it's like a coat;
and if the coat is yours, it has a tear
like a wide mouth and when the mouth begins
to draw the wind, it's like a trumpeter
and when the trumpet blows, it blows like millions...
and this, my love, when millions come and go
beyond the need of us, is like a trick;
and when the trick begins, it's like a toe
tip-toeing on a rope, which is like luck;
and when the luck begins, it's like a wedding,
which is like love, which is like everything.

Alice Oswald

We feel a pleasant sense of surprise when similar sounds are unexpectedly linked and their relationship comes to seem somehow inevitable.

As leaders, repetition can help us to create connection and resonance. It enables us to repeat or recast a point to ensure it has been heard and understood; to stress something important. We can use repetition to reflect and endorse what we hear from others too.

We know that our messages have been heard and understood when we start to hear them come, unbidden and rephrased, from others around the organisation.

Rhyme

Poetic language also draws heavily on the repetition of specific sounds, known as rhyme. Rhyming isolates and repeats a natural sub unit of a word in a new context. Rhymes link meanings through similarities in sound; the pattern of poetic rhyme serves to stitch several lines together.

Robert Frost portrayed poetry without rhyme is being like *tennis without a net* (although perhaps he never played squash!).

Prosody has three types of sound repetition:

* Alliteration - repetition of the initial sounds of words or syllables: '*sultry, silken sentences*'
* Assonance - repetition or internal vowel sounds (vowel rhyme), and
* Consonance - repetition of internal or end consonant sounds

As well as having an aesthetic component, rhyme can help with recall of specific words. In particular, alliterations retrieve similar sounding words and phrases from a person's memory, making them a useful tool for comprehension and memorisation of both poetry and prose.

Repetition is often used in oratory to stress a particular point, and to create a sense of inevitability and flow. As leaders, we can capitalise on the power of repetition to reinforce important values and messages. Doing this creatively, so that messages are retold, rephrased, and subtly echoed (as we see in poetic approaches) rather than recited monotonously, will ensure that people stay interested and curious, rather than feeling patronised and tuning out. Such *rhyming* can create a sense of coherence not only within our words, but in images and actions too; it will bring a sense of trueness and fit to everything we say and do.

Although end rhyme (at the end of lines) is the most well-known pattern, anaphora (at the beginning of lines) and internal rhyme (within a line or lines) are important techniques to consider when creating a poem.

Poetic rhyme relies heavily on assonance, or vowel rhyme, but true rhymes -

house and mouse, for example - will also repeat the consonant sounds of words. Poets also use eye rhyme - words that look the same but sound different; such as rough and dough, or from Shakespeare's Sonnet 116:

> *If this be error and upon me proved,*
> *I never writ, nor no man ever loved.*

and slant rhyme - such as heart and dark, faces and houses, lover and brother. In such rhymes the connections are more subtle and intriguing.

> *It was a hard thing to undo this knot.*
> *The rainbow shines, but only in the thought*
> *Of him that looks. Yet not in that alone,*
> *For who makes rainbows by invention?*

Gerard Manley Hopkins

Repetitive Forms

Most classical western poetry is written in rhyming lines and regular metre, often in a set pattern or 'fixed form'. Rhyming schemes can be interlocked; examples of this include the rondeau, sestina and sonnet. Many sonnets (such as Wordsworth's *London, 1802*) have a nested rhyme scheme - abba - which creates a kind of embrace, emphasising the poem's intimacy. Michaela Ridgway subverts this form subtly in her sonnet-like *Ablutions*.

Ablutions

> *I've chosen Bach's cello suites - the Casals' -*
> *and opened the window above the bath.*
> *For the first time in months, a kind of faith*
> *rises in me, like the slow hoist of sails*
> *or a semiquaver's climb through intervals*
> *up the ledger-line ladder of its staff;*

it's not a game of blindfold in the dark –
it's like learning to see again with braille.
It's my still-warm pyjamas in a pile
on the floor; how I slip myself in, toe-
first, to water. The way the body drifts,
forgets itself sometimes, travels miles
and how the pulse this heart emits, although
submerged, will sound the body home; it's this.

Michaela Ridgway

A number of fixed poetic forms rely on the repetition of whole lines, both throughout the poem and as a final refrain. Examples include the villanelle, pantoum and ghazal. These forms each have a particular feel.

The villanelle form (such as Elizabeth Bishop's *One Art*) supports a progressive surge of tone and intensity. In contrast, a pantoum (such as *Command* by Rachel Barenblat - page 106) has an incantatory feel and is well suited to instruction or to the circular, perhaps even obsessive, exploration of a single thought; like a mobius strip.

A ghazal (such as Heather McHugh's below) is a playful form of autonomous stanzas which share a rhymed refrain. The final couplet usually includes a maker's mark, using the author's name or a derivation of its meaning.

Ghazal of the Better-Unbegun

Too volatile, am I? too voluble? too much a word-person?
I blame the soup: I'm a primordially
stirred person.

Two pronouns and a vehicle was Icarus with wings.
The apparatus of his selves made an ab-

surd person.

The sound I make is sympathy's: sad dogs are tied afar.
But howling I become an ever more un-
heard person.

I need a hundred more of you to make a likelihood.
The mirror's not convincing-- that at-best in-
ferred person.

As time's revealing gets revolting, I start looking out.
Look in and what you see is one unholy
blurred person.

The only cure for birth one doesn't love to contemplate.
Better to be an unsung song, an unoc-
curred person.

McHugh, you'll be the death of me -- each self and second studied!
Addressing you like this, I'm halfway to the
third person.

Heather McHugh

Putting it all Together

A poet uses prosody to create a particular style and inflection that supports their message. These are conscious and deliberate choices. The poet is required to think carefully about the words they use and their sequence; to enroll words not just for their meaning but for euphony, to help fuse all the elements of a poem into a seamless whole.

Seamus Heaney's poem *Personal Helicon,* for example, has a formal *abab* rhyming scheme, along with many partial rhymes, tons of consonance, some examples of word repetition, and a sly reflection of the writer (ghazal-like) in the final stanza.

As leaders we need to attune to people's needs and set the tone in our organisations with similar care.

Personal Helicon
for Michael Longley

As a child, they could not keep me from wells
And old pumps with buckets and windlasses.
I loved the dark drop, the trapped sky, the smells
Of waterweed, fungus and dank moss.
One, in a brickyard, with a rotted board top.
I savoured the rich crash when a bucket
Plummeted down at the end of a rope.
So deep you saw no reflection in it.
A shallow one under a dry stone ditch
Fructified like any aquarium.
When you dragged out long roots from the soft mulch
A white face hovered over the bottom.
Others had echoes, gave back your own call
With a clean new music in it. And one
Was scaresome, for there, out of ferns and tall
Foxgloves, a rat slapped across my reflection.
Now, to pry into roots, to finger slime,
To stare, big-eyed Narcissus, into some spring
Is beneath all adult dignity. I rhyme
To see myself, to set the darkness echoing.

Seamus Heaney

11

LEADING WITH RHYTHM: THE CADENCE OF WORK

Our biological rhythms are the symphony of the cosmos, music embedded deep within us to which we dance, even when we can't name the tune.

Deepak Chopra

The Rhythm of Life

Every living thing has rhythm and flow. Atoms and molecules consist of waves and vibrations. Living organisms have cycles of activity and rest, and their physiological functions have rhythmic oscillations. On a bigger scale, ecosystems and civilizations have cyclical patterns of energy flow and growth or decline.

Even our planet has daily and seasonal rhythms as it spins around the sun on its axis. We are immersed in a natural symphony of rhythms, and organisations, made up of people and the work they do, are no exception. As leaders we must observe the right rhythm and pace for work.

Aristotle was one of the earliest writers to describe society and organisations in dramaturgical terms, in which rhythm (and dialog) play a pivotal role. He thought rhythm *"the greatest of pleasurable accessories of Tragedy".*

Rhythm is made up of novelty and change, and a tension between order and chaos. Rhythm can be predictable, or can consist of chaotic patterns that refuse to stay still. It can offer predictability and stasis, or provide space for improvisation, experimentation and change. We see rhythm at work, in the form of daily, weekly, monthly and yearly routines; cycles of growth (and decay); hiring and firing. Some rhythms are planned, and some are emergent.

What Rhythm is For

We are rhythmic animals, with a neural system that is *grooved* for sound. Our exposure to rhythm starts in the womb, with our mother's heart beat and voice forming our acoustic experience. As a result we are born with strong capacities for being expressive in time; babies are innately musical, and have an excellent sense of rhythm. Professor Colwyn Trevarthen has studied the interactions of mothers and babies in the early months. [21] Even when a mother is not singing to a baby, she tends to speak in a musical way, with rising and falling tone and inflections, and a clear rhythm. And perhaps more astonishing, the baby responds in sound and gesture, often exactly in time with the pulse and bar structure of her sounds. Trevarthen says that they 'get in the groove' like jazz musicians improvising.

We appeal to babies' rhythmic sensibility in the timeless format of bedtime lullabies, most of which are in a time signature (6/8) which creates a swinging motion and a hypnotic quality.

Rhythm also helps trigger memory. Historically, in a time before people could read and write, rhythm (and rhyme) helped people to remember stories, and metrical music is used today in dementia clinics to help elderly people to recall decades old facts about their lives.

Rhythm can also be used to alter consciousness, as for example in traditional drumming ceremonies. Rhythm acts as an *auditory driver*, and can induce trance as normal brainwave patterns shift to follow an external rhythm. Whilst most clearly seen in the forms of drumming and dance, all rhythm can alter consciousness, and it is an important part of many rituals and organised social activities, including organisational events. It might be argued that any account of culture or organisation is incomplete unless it takes account of rhythm and our innate responses to it.

The Cadence of Work

Rhythmic movement is a natural consequence of the body doing physical work, and maximises muscular efficiency. The size and weight of any work load (such as a hammer) controls the rhythm or speed of a worker's action. Because of this, traditional tools tend to be of a particular size, designed to maximise muscular efficiency for the task.

When two or more workers are involved, they fall into a shared rhythm. This property of two rhythmic patterns adjusting to match each other is known as entrainment, and is seen for example in the swinging of clock pendulums, the physical actions of co-workers, and the menstrual cycles of women who live together. Entrainment has a strong role in channelling and coordinating human energy, and there is a close link between rhythmic music and work output. For example in 1955, psychologist P. C. Wason observed workers at the Cusson's factory doing a strange rhythmic dance to the factory's piped music as they packed soap. The greater the *jigging* the greater was their efficiency. [22]

Perhaps this increased efficiency is part of why physical work across the globe is often accompanied by singing or chanting, from the spiritual songs sung by ditch diggers in the Caribbean to the Hebridean *waulking* songs sung by women as they soften home woven cloth. Sometimes, as seen in Kodo drumming, people not only move, but breathe as one.

Although more immediately apparent in physical work, rhythm is an important factor in productivity of any kind.

Command

A perpetual fire shall be kept burning on the altar, not to go out. - Lev. 6:6

First you dress in linen
then scoop out the ashes.
Stop and wash with water,
then you change your garments

and scoop out the ashes.
Lather, rinse, repeat;
then you change your garments.
No one said it was easy.

Lather, rinse, repeat;
out here in the wilderness
no one said it was easy
to keep the fire burning.

Out here in the wilderness
there's little wood to scavenge
to keep the fire burning
all night until morning.

There's little wood to scavenge
and you want perpetual motion
all night until morning—
that's the ritual of the offering.

You want perpetual motion
but fires don't burn forever
and the ritual of the offering
is this lesson from the waters.

Fires don't burn forever
(except for that holy pillar)
so take a lesson from the waters
and the reeds you sludged across.

Remember that holy pillar
like a beacon in the darkness
and the reeds you sludged across
each shaky step toward freedom.

Like a beacon in the darkness
God's instructions on this are clear:
each shaky step toward freedom
keeps the fire burning.

God's instructions on this are clear.
Stop and wash with water.
Keep the fire burning.
First you dress in linen.

Rachel Barenblat

Rhythm as Social Discourse

According to academic Richard Rogers, "*rhythm is a form of discourse central to social organisation*". [23] Our rhythmic sensibilities help us to distinguish music from noise; order from chaos. Rogers 'hears' rhythm as one means of enacting or performing *organisation*; one way in which order is made of our worlds. Rhythmic discourse and bodily engagement occurs in all human interactions: household routines, local or religious traditions, seasonal planting and harvesting, corporate meeting schedules and musical improvisation.

Organisation is everywhere. It can feel stifling or freeing. A challenge for us as leaders is to develop a rhythmic structure or *organisation* that acts as a safety net, yet allows freedom - much as the musical structure of free jazz enables players to improvise and innovate in a cohesive and coordinated way.

Rhythm in Speech

Rhythm in human language is a musical quality produced by the repetition of stressed and unstressed syllables. The rhythm of everyday conversation is a result of cadence - of the natural pattern of sounds of words - and is created unconsciously.

We often mirror another's rhythm of speech and even the numbers of syllables we use, which creates resonance, and allows us to "tune in" when listening to one another. For example, when lovers talk to each other, they will synchronise their postures and gestures, mirroring the other. Rhythmic mirroring can also be used consciously in conversations, and builds connection as we each speak.

The notion of turn taking and predetermined structure in conversation is heightened in theatre and novels, in rituals or ceremonies, and in organisations, for example in formal meetings and regular planned communications. Ordinary conversation, in contrast, is far less ping-pong. It involves an emergent approach to turn-taking, complete with interruptions and digressions. It is pervasively interactive and improvisational.

Rhythm in Poetry

Rhythm is a (perhaps *the*) key component of music and dance, and is present in all voice/language based arts (written or spoken). But it is in poetry that the driving beat of language meets meaning. Poetry occupies the intersection of rhythm and language; connects the physical pulse of our interactions in the world with our primary means of making sense of it.

In poetry, rhythm is the patterned repetition of features of sound and language. The presence of rhythmic patterns conveys movement, heightens emotional response and often gives a sense of balance.

Poetry mimics the waves of breath (or inspiration) that accompany speech. Indeed, poetic rhythms are sometimes ascribed to units of breath. In his essay *Projective Verse*, poet and critic Charles Olson suggests: *"And the line comes (I swear it) from the breath, from the breathing of the man who writes, at the moment that he writes."* [24]

The Makers

Who can remember back to the first poets,
The greatest ones, greater even than Orpheus?
No one has remembered that far back
Or now considers, among the artifacts,
And bones and cantilevered inference
The past is made of, those first and greatest poets,
So lofty and disdainful of renown
They left us not a name to know them by.
They were the ones that in whatever tongue
Worded the world, that were the first to say
Star, water, stone, that said the visible
And made it bring invisibles to view
In wind and time and change, and in the mind
Itself that minded the hitherto idiot world
And spoke the speechless world and sang the towers
Of the city into the astonished sky.
They were the first great listeners, attuned

To interval, relationship, and scale,
The first to say above, beneath, beyond,
Conjurors with love, death, sleep, with bread and wine,
Who having uttered vanished from the world
Leaving no memory but the marvelous
Magical elements, the breathing shapes
And stops of breath we build our Babels of.

Howard Nemerov

We use the term *prosody* to describe the metre, rhythm, and intonation of poetry. Rhythm and metre are different, although closely related:

- *Metre* is the definitive pattern established for a verse and is one method of organising a poem's rhythm, using elements of stress, duration, or number of syllables per line.
- *Rhythm* is the actual sound that results from a line of poetry.

So, metre is the plan and rhythm is the experience. The metre of a line may be identified as *iambic*, but a full description of the rhythm would note where the language causes the reader to pause or accelerate (the phrase *'hitherto idiot'* in Nemerov's poem, for example) and how the metre interacts with other elements of the language, some of them speaker- or reader-specific. The rhythm will be subtly different each time a poem is read. This interaction of a given metrical pattern with other aspects of sound in a poem produces a counterpoint in the writing.

Linguist Isabelle Guaïtella uses metre and rhythm to describe different flavours of speech: directive or mechanical; and transformative or engaging. [25] A metric tendency focusses on timing and the regulation of intervals. A rhythmic one focuses instead on the production of events and our perception of them. We might argue that management talk has a metric sensibility and leadership a rhythmic one.

For Rudolf Steiner, founder of anthroposophy, rhythm was about action. He wrote about the power of music to link hearing and thinking. There are similar links in poetry. Steiner suggested that the centre of music is harmony (we would say *tone* in poetry), as it goes directly to feeling; to the heart of human experience. Melody (or *vocabulary*) carries that feeling into thinking, by making the head accessible to feelings; rhythm directs the feeling into willing, the body, and hence to action. Poetic leadership connects ideas, feelings and action.

William Carlos Williams defined the movement of a poem as *"intrinsic, undulant, a physical more than a literary character."* [26] Prosody is the energy of that poem, the thumping cadence of the poem's engine that creates pace and momentum. It is the drum beat of rhythm that drives each line forward toward and beyond the cliff edge of each line break and stanza end. Well executed, a poem's rhythm gives it energy and authenticity, however unusual. We see the *tenor* and the *vehicle* of this energy in Dylan Thomas' poem *The Force That through the Green Fuse Drives the Flower.*

Choices of Rhythm and Form

Rhythm in poetry may be obvious or muted. Whilst some forms of poetry have a specific rhythmic pattern, others, such as free verse, tend to use the more natural cadences of speech. Free verse often has underlying rhythmical patterns emerging from its sonic features, that, although not strictly "regular", do create an impression of unity.

Rhythmic contemporary verse is sometimes called accentual-syllabic because it is made up of metrical units each containing a set number of accents (stresses) as well as a set number of syllables in each line. The description of these patterns is known as *scansion*. The terms of scansion describe the names of the different *feet* (combinations of stressed or unstressed syllables), and the varying line lengths. Although useful for describing the underlying structure of a poem, scansion is too heavy handed for describing the subtle nuances of language's rhythms.

The traditional prosody of a language tends to use phonetic features that are familiar and immediately audible to native speakers. The English language is more heavily stressed than many, and so English poetic metre depends on stress, rather than on the number of syllables as, for example, in traditional Greek, Latin and Arabic poetry. The most commonly used metre in English rhetoric (for example by politicians and in some forms of theatre) is iambic, which is particularly reflective of ordinary speech. It is easy and natural to say, sounding almost like a heart beat.

Arise, fair sun, and kill the envious moon,
Who is already sick and pale with grief

from ***Romeo and Juliet***, William Shakespeare

Slavish adherence to any one metre can switch us off after a while. An alternative is to structure a poem around a metre and line length, and then depart from it and play against it as needed in order to create effect. These deviations call attention to themselves and quicken or slow the pace at which the poem is read.

'Hearing' The Rhythm of Organisations

There are many different kinds of rhythm that operate within our work environment. Corporate rhythms can be seasonal, cyclical, linear or non-linear, mechanical or more organic. Some are authoritarian (or centered) rhythms - that discipline, control, and reproduce an order - and others are a more democratic dance - that subvert, resist, and enact a different order. Some rhythms emerge from within, others (such as national programmes) are imposed from outside.

Effective leaders are aware of the rhythms at play within their organisation, and know how to read them, ride them, and shift them when necessary. They can interact with organisational rhythms to increase productivity and allegiance. As Margaret Wheatley writes, mindful leaders *"look for patterns of movement over time, and focus on the qualities of rhythm, flow, direction, and shape, on networks of relationships and energy flows".* [27]

Empowering leaders accomplish their goals through other people by creating an overall plan with a clear rhythm and trusting that each person will perform *in sync* with it. Understanding timing and pace enables the leader to bring together the energy of the group and give it direction and movement into the future. Being in touch with rhythm comes from experience, and from listening with all our senses and intuition.

Uses of Rhythm

Rhythm, including timing, pace and stress, is core to our experience of work, and of leading or being led. A successful leader can engage the rhythms of human interaction to coordinate and focus individual and collective activities; to put the stress where it is needed. Great performances of any kind usually have a natural rhythm. A co-ordinated flow can make any action (whether diving, playing the piano, chopping wood or throwing a pot) look easy.

Effective leaders are able to use rhythm within their organisations; to help people to join smoothly in the flow of events, and to work productively with coordinated thoughts and actions. They use rhythm to energise work and build confidence in the leadership team.

Shaping the rhythm of an organisation helps us to speak to people's emotions; through it we can connect with them, and shape the energy and pace of work and information that passes between people. Rhythm helps us to focus, connect and be *in the moment*. A steady rhythm provides stability and creates a sense of team work and order; it provides something regular and predictable for people. However, as we saw in relation to poetic metre, an unvarying or mechanical rhythm can be overly dogmatic. To energise and engage, rhythm needs to breathe. It must also allow freedom for people to improvise and syncopate.

People will be looking to the rhythm to tell them not only what to do, but whether they belong. In any busy environment, people may need to adapt in order to fit in with the rhythm of the people around them, but there are limits to how much they will be willing or comfortable to change. We all have our own natural rhythms. Some feel comfortable in rapid changing environment and are easily bored if things stay the same. Others prefer stability and certainty. When rhythms are mismatched, a *dissonance* can arise. For example, in a fast paced environment, managers may feel that change is too slow, whilst people working in the same organisation may find the number and pace of changes too frenetic. A poetic leader will take these factors into account.

Creating New Rhythms

Rhythm will inevitably be present whether it is crafted or simply emerges. A challenge for us as leaders, then, is to create the right kind of rhythm and flow in our organisations and to help people to hear it and to work with it. This is ever more critical if staff are struggling with workload, are burned out or have lost their 'spark'.

A clear organisational rhythm, enacted through a cohesive set of communications, events, images, and employee experiences, can help to develop trust and meaningful relationships. There needs to be a good mix of regular events and flexible responses: a well-planned series of ordinary actions - meaningful meetings, reporting mechanisms and events - alongside extraordinary happenings designed to maximise connection and creative thinking or in response to specific issues - such as awaydays, emergency meetings and *floor walking*.

As we will see later in this chapter, disruptive rhythms can be useful. However, if events (such as meetings) are frequently reactive and problem based, the prevalent metre of the organisation will be problem-driven.

It is vital to have a distinct rhythm and tone that is fit for the purpose in mind. Too often organisational activities and communications merge into an indistinct mass. Classically, the focus of business versus strategic, or day-to-day versus emergency, gets blurred, with the uncomfortable result that everything feels equally urgent and important, and we can't see the wood for the trees.

The Wood-Pile (extract)

Out walking in the frozen swamp one gray day,
I paused and said, 'I will turn back from here.
No, I will go on farther—and we shall see.'
The hard snow held me, save where now and then
One foot went through. The view was all in lines
Straight up and down of tall slim trees
Too much alike to mark or name a place by
So as to say for certain I was here
Or somewhere else: I was just far from home.

Robert Frost

Designing for Rhythm

Rhythm is closely related to structure or form, and physicists such as Frijof Capra believe that rhythmic models in nature can help us understand the passages between structure and rhythm, vital components in organisation(s). The resonant frequency of a system is closely related to the distances between its constituent parts. The physical design of the work environment, and the pace and pattern of systems and processes can help or hinder departmental rhythm. Subtle changes can have a big impact on productivity and engagement. Long distances to the meeting spaces; slow response times and decision making; isolation from other team members; obsolete or slow technology - many controllable factors can block flow and rhythm.

We sometimes see problems (discontinuities) where there is a significant difference in the natural rhythms of teams needing to work together. For example, the rhythm and pace of an hospital Accident and Emergency

Department is very different to that of a Social Service Assessment Team. Rhythm can be a cause of tension when the two need to collaborate.

We need to fully understand the interdependency of structure and rhythm if we wish to master this aspect of organisational life. This is especially true when we think about the *human factors* at times of organisational change. By thinking about rhythm, we can design processes and structures that amplify the pulse of our organisations.

Rhythm as Disruption

People have an innate human need to participate in rhythmic processes. Although, in some settings, we may wish to limit any emergent rhythms, with their possibility of disrupting events, it is usually better to engage the willing participation of people by incorporating their chosen rhythm into the whole. It is important to capitalise on the fact that people think and express themselves differently. The differences in rhythm that people bring are not so much problems, but opportunities for action.

As well as the need to find a unifying rhythm, it is important to harness the transformative potential of non-dominant and resistant rhythms, as found in jazz, african polyrhythms and beat poetry (such as that of Ginsberg and Ferlinghetti). These can provide a counterpoint and challenge or stimulus, but are not the same as a permanent discontinuity (i.e. a rhythm that jumps levels; a barrier that people have to work round).

Jacques Attali explores the power of subversion rhythm in his book *Noise: The Political Economy of Music.* Against a backdrop of order and harmony, any particular music either affirms the status quo or subverts it through the production of noise. Such noise is primarily either destructive or creative.

Sometimes a leader will want to vary an organisational rhythm, to add interest and excitement, or to stimulate new thinking. Such arrhythmias or dysrhythmias may open up new possibilities and creative solutions to familiar problems. Organisational development activities - awaydays and conferences -

are deliberate attempts to break the normal rhythm and enable people to think more creatively about themselves and their work.

Rhythmic disruptions and breaks from form are used frequently in poetry (and far more deliberately than in prose) in order to make a point or draw attention to a word, an image or an idea.

ECG

Your heart's signature in lime
p-q-r-s-t then curlicue,
like signing endless cheques apace;
as if your love were waving too,
or signalling distress in mime.
As adoration starts to waver
muscle cells still undulate,
beating out each second's grace;
half-moon valves still syncopate,
now minim, rest, now semi-quaver.
A cipher in each peak and trough,
scratched into your cardiograph;
to read the runes within the trace
I need no help from nursing staff –
hearing the rhythm's stutter's clue enough.

Beth Somerford

Rhythm & Change

Rhythm can act as a powerful change agent. As Professors Bob and Janet Denhardt suggest in The Dance of Leadership: "*The beats provide the obvious structure and constitute moments of stability, but, between each accent, there is an open space, an opportunity, begging to be filled.*" [28] Rhythm exemplifies the tension between stability and change that is the essence of life. In the space that follows a moment of stability, one of a million things might happen. Change occurs in the breathing space between beats; in the hesitation, the suspended moment, between THIS now THIS now THIS.

Stability is in the beat, the accent, the thing, the light, the yang;

Change is in the breath, the space, the opportunity, the dark, the yin.

The rhythms of work are characterised by a tension between certainty and uncertainty; reality and possibility. It is the leader's role to help the group move between these, gathering energy and commitment in both the knowing and the unknowing.

The purpose of rhythm in poetry, according to W. B. Yeats, *"is to prolong the moment of contemplation, the moment when we are both asleep and awake, which is the one moment of creation, by hushing us with an alluring monotony, while it holds us waking by variety, to keep us in that state of perhaps real trance, in which the mind liberated from the pressure of the will is unfolded in symbols".* [29]   So, then, will a poetic leader follow the breathing rhythm of ebb-and-flow; give-and-take; lead-and-follow.

Rhythm is part of the unique signature of individuals as well as of organisations. Our gestures, movement, speech, even our cardiogram, identify us; express essential things about us. We can choose the kind of energy we use as leaders, in our own pursuits and in how we relate to others. Gabrielle Roth, creator of Five Rhythms dance, describes five different rhythms of human movement: flowing, staccato, chaos, lyrical and stillness. Although we may feel most at home in one of the rhythms, there is a time for every rhythm (both for us and for the organisation we are in). Being able to consciously change from one rhythm – or type of energy – to another is an invaluable leadership skill.

A leader's sense of timing is crucial too - seeing the openings or opportunities and choosing the best time to act; to use the rhythm's momentum. Great timing requires us to sense the rhythm around us. If we are out of touch we might miss the beat.

12

SHAPE MAKING:
STRUCTURE, FORM & SPACE

the shape of words like the shadows
of doves, settling

From *What The Translator Knows,* Jane Griffiths

The Poem as a Thing

Literary theorists and critics tend to approach poetry in one of two ways. The first is to concentrate on the poet, following the idea that poetry is primarily an expression of the poet's emotion (as Wordsworth said, *"the spontaneous overflow of powerful feeling"*). The second is to discuss the poem itself as a made thing; a *poiesis*. Here, the poet is as a "maker" of meanings with words; a craftsman working with the content and form of poetry.

When we talk about leadership, we usually focus on the leader - what kind of person they are; whether they are 'good' or 'bad' - rather than what they create. In this chapter, we look at the impact of shape, structure and form in poetry and leadership.

The Shape of Things

Form in poetry is the arrangement, manner or method used to organise and convey its content. There is a wide choice of patterns, from fixed forms of layout, rhyming scheme or rhythm (as seen in the poetry of Dante, Goethe and Yeats), to unrhymed blank verse (used by Shakespeare and Wordsworth), to free form poetry (such as that of Charles Bukowski and Carolyn Forché).

Form can also be specific for a genre of poetry - from the sparse lines of a haiku, or the lush rhymes of victorian romantic verse, to the complex rhythms and alliteration of epic skaldic poetry. Poets today are likely to draw from - and even combine - diverse forms.

Form is a key part of *the way said*. The poet needs to make choices about shape and form carefully, as it should not only reflect the purpose and style of a poem, but will give the reader clues about meaning and tone. When a poem's tone and shape fits with its theme, it lends credence to its particular circumstance. Such a poem has an overall sense of congruence, *showing* rather than *telling* us its message. A form that fits its context is also one that we perceive as being beautiful and enabling, not restrictive. The shape of a well crafted poem is not at odds with the poem's creative purpose. As sociologist

Lewis Mumford says, *"The fact that order and creativity are complementary has been basic to man's cultural development; for he has to internalize order to be able to give external form to his creativity."* [30]

Formality & Fluidity

But art must conceal art, and form must not be overdone. As David Morley suggests: *"Form provides a "pattern" for the poem, but is usually most effective when it is the least obvious. Poems must seem to be inevitable."* [31] Morley describes a process of playing with different forms until a poem either 'clicks' into the right form, or decides that it wants to be 'free' verse, adding, *"The move into free verse is always a pleasant surprise for a poem that has passed through so many cages and narrow ways. And such a poem bears the voice-print of strictness and discipline while also appearing to be merely spoken, inevitably, as if improvised on the spot."* Such poetry enjoys the freedom on the *other side* of restriction.

We need a certain amount of structure so we can be free. Complete chaos is paralysing. *'Restriction is liberation'* (as Igor Stravinsky said). But the structure of a poem, an organisation or a process is simply a vessel or vehicle for its overriding purpose; a leader must provide people with a framework within which to operate, not a straightjacket.

Although structure and form are the enablers of rhythm, we should not get too hung up on them - the rhythm must have space; must live. One of the most common failings in organisational change programmes is too great a focus on structure and process, and not enough on the human factors of change.

Adaptability and flexibility are key. Typical organisations exhibit turnover of staff, frequent restructuring of teams and business units, and time limited task-and-finish or matrix-based activities. The structure that is fit for purpose one day will be archaic the next. If we are to maintain motivation and engagement, processes must not become monotonous. A degree of variety in pattern - of deviation from form - will help to keep people's interest.

Layout & Look

A poem's form has a unique interplay between space and time; between its visual shape and its auditory signature, spoken in time. Many poetic devices play on this mediation between the written and the oral. In end rhyme for example, the written unit of the line is reinforced by the aural repetition of the rhyme; the rhyme is made possible by the layout.

Shape is part of what *embodies* words fully. As I. A. Richards suggests, the sound of the words in the ear and the feel of the words imaginarily spoken are what give them full body, and it is with words' full bodies, rather than their printed signs, that the poet works.

Storm Warning

Inside the conch, enormous night rages. Trees sway like prophets
lost in their visions and the world is horse, wild hoarse, chasing itself
through empty streets where cardboard makes love to lamp posts and
houses crouch like beaten women. I have slipped over the wet lip of the
windowsill, an ash fleck posted into echoes. Darkness is freshly sliced,
a raw wound unfolding; I will prove a match for it, small shell roaring large.

Catherine Ayres

The look of a poem as a whole often adds meaning or depth to the words used. Historically important in the more graphic languages such as Arabic, Hebrew and Chinese, visual elements have become more deliberate in western poetry over the last century.

American poetry, sometimes identified as a poetics of landscape, has a particularly intimate relationship with its visual element. Walt Whitman's expansiveness, for example, has much to do with the relation of his long lines to the blank space of the page.

Why I seldom talk to strange women at parties

It
started
as a
dribble
erratic
tickling
this way and
that
like a spring
in a mountain
cave a slight
tinkle flowing
over lips of rock
beneath flipping bats
of eyelids and other
facial exclamation marks
I liked the sound the flow
in the speech the ribbons
and currents wending in the air
moving in rushing waves sounding
syllables like poetry in water music
until slowly the build the head of stream
started to overwhelm and I felt cowed
and unsteady beaten by the force a swimmer
against a tide I could not overcome and so I turned
thrashing in the noise and swam striking for the shore
swam swam violently for the safety of the silent gaping door

Marc Woodward

Some poets make the placement of the lines on the page an integral part of the poem's composition, using the verbal equivalent of artist Paul Klee's *taking a line for a walk*. The effect of visual presentation may complement or cut across the poem's rhythm, accentuating it's meaning or strangeness. The most obvious form of visual presentation is in concrete poetry, in which the shape of the poem on the page somehow reflects the poem's content, such as Marc Woodward's example.

Just as the interplay of visual and oral goes to create the full 'body' of a *word*, so a well formed *poem* is fully embodied, its visual presence an integral part of its language. So too the leader's embodied language; their posture, gestures and visual image - not just their speech - constitute a vital part of their gravitas; of their overall standing.

Lines & Stanzas

Most poetry is separated into lines on a page, often based on a metric scheme or end-rhyme pattern. Lines of poetry are often organised into stanzas or '*rooms*'. In formal structures, the stanzas are likely to have a specific number of lines, for example couplets, terzas or quatrains, and an associated scheme of some kind. Each stanza may also form a complete stream of thought, or part of a story. Less formal poems may be organised into verse paragraphs, with a looser collection of rhythms, alliterations, and rhymes gelling each paragraph.

In many poetic forms, such as the ghazal and the villanelle, stanzas are interlocking, meaning that structural elements (such as the rhyming scheme) of one stanza determine those of succeeding stanzas.

The poem ECG (on page 116) contains an interlocking envelope rhyme scheme (ABCBA, DECED, FGCGF, with F and G also being half rhymes). In some poetic traditions, such as the skaldic poetry of Iceland and Scandinavia, the structure is even more complex and strict.

The lines and stanzas in a poem make it easier to follow the overall theme and content, and can strengthen any rhythmic or rhyming scheme. They can help to create a sense of coherence and inevitability, particularly important when the content is surprising or includes an unusual combination of themes. In management-speak, lines and stanzas can help to 'chunk the elephant'; to divide a complex process, problem or project into bite-sized pieces.

Punctuation

Another means of order that can help us navigate our written language, is punctuation. A report or a book without punctuation marks would be anarchic; like a society without rules. Punctuation marks are lynchpins of language, helping to organise words and thoughts, and to modulate flow and create rhythm.

In prose, punctuation marks have an overwhelmingly semantic function, changing the meaning of a sentence through the movement of tiny marks on the page. But they are also fundamentally marks of oral delivery, and hearing readers tend to associate each punctuation mark with a particular acoustic image.

In poetry, punctuation hovers between visual, aural and syntactic functions. It helps poets navigate the space between the written and the oral, translating words on a page into an aural experience close to the one the poet heard when she created the poem. Punctuation helps to signal where the reader should pause or pay attention; the more punctuation, the slower we read a poem.

Poetry tends to have less punctuation than prose, and a poet will often use spaces or line breaks to do the same job with less disturbance of the flow or visual simplicity of the poem. Some writers argue that less-is-more, and that we should use the minimum punctuation necessary to convey the sense and tone we intend. Others see punctuation as an integral part of the poem, and our visual experience of it on the page. Indeed, there is a poem called 'thorn' that consists of a single comma.

Punctuation is related to poetic style. Didactic poetry tends to rely on punctuation marks to ensure clarity, whereas haiku or block poems do not. The use of punctuation is also part of poet's own individuality. Emily Dickinson used a wild selection of dashes, question marks and exclamation marks in her poetry, and often capitalised first letters, whereas e e cummings (and Marc Woodward earlier in this chapter) used very little punctuation.

The placement of punctuation has an important effect in poetry. Punctuation at the end of lines (end-stops) cause us to pause and stress the last word of the line, especially if accentuated by end-rhymes too.

Bright Star

Bright Star, would I were as stedfast as thou art—
Not in lone splendor hung aloft the night,
And watching, with eternal lids apart,
Like nature's patient, sleepless Eremite,

Keats

In contrast, *enjambment* (from the French for "straddling") occurs when a phrase, and often an idea, in one line continues in the next line or verse. Enjambment encourages us to move on without pausing, and creates a stream of consciousness, sometimes with a sense of urgency or disorder.

April is the cruelest month, breeding
Lilacs out of the dead land, mixing
Memory and desire, stirring
Dull roots with spring rain.

from *The Waste Land* by T.S Eliot

Line breaks can also help to stress a particular word and create a momentary suspension of perception.

> ---listen: there's a hell
> Of a good universe next door; let's go.

from *pity this busy monster, manunkind* by ee cummings

and

> The wind flung a magpie away and a black-
> back gull bent like an iron bar slowly....

from *Wind* by Ted Hughes

The minute marks and actions of punctuation have a big impact on our senses and understanding. These small things matter. So too do the punctuating gestures that we make as leaders: eye contact; a nod; a touch; saying "yes", and "thank you"; starting an email with a greeting. In such simple ways we signal our intentions and the tone of our connections.

The patterns of our working lives - of events, processes, meetings, reporting cycles - are symbolic and evocative. The choices we make to finalise decisions and close debates, or hold issues over for further consideration - the end stopping or enjambment of agenda items - are subtle but important. It is dangerous both to repeatedly defer a nebulous problem and to make knee jerk decisions on familiar issues.

Endings are crucial too. As well as its closing thought or sentiment, the final mark of a poem, and the space that follows, will signify clearly that it has come to an end. This sense of closure and completion is important. Neither a poem, a speech or a corridor interaction should just fizzle out.

Pausing for Breath

The poetic form has many means of imposing pauses. Poetry often encourages or requires us to read slowly, to breathe, to stop and think, and listen. Much of its power lies in the relationship - the contrast - between the words and the white space of the page.

Thirty spokes meet at a nave;
Because of the hole we may use the wheel.
Clay is moulded into a vessel;
Because of the hollow we may use the cup.
Walls are built around a hearth;
Because of the doors we may use the house.
Thus tools come from what exists,
But use from what does not.

from the ***Tao Te Ching,*** Chapter 11, Lao Tzu

Space is one means by which a poet prolongs meaning. As J. Hillis Miller writes of William Carlos Williams' confessional poem *Asphodel, That Greeny Flower,* "*The poem is also the space of language, of a murmuring speech which the poet prolongs defiantly and yet precariously, with infinite gentleness, against time and death*". [32]

And so
                         with fear in my heart
                                        I drag it out
       and keep on talking
                    for I dare not stop.
                              Listen while I talk on
       against time.

White space on the page is the visual or physical equivalent of silence. Just as a poem's life lies in the breath between the words, so is space - to rest, pause and think - a key tool in the leader's toolkit. We need respite from intensity; contrast between doing and not doing. Calm, white space is the realm of the imagination.

Effective leadership is both measured and spacious; it provides for down time and reflection. Even in a busy environment, when pressures to make decisions are great, we may need to buy a little time - to create a breathing space within which further information gathering and investigation can take place, in order to arrive, ultimately, at a better decision. We all need space and time to think our best thoughts.

Claude Debussy defined music as *"the space between the notes"*. A classic problem, especially in large organisations of autonomous professionals, is that everyone plays their notes, but no one conducts the spaces between. A leader needs to regard the whole, and especially the spaces that no-one else is attending to.

One of the ironies of great leadership is that we have to be able to let go. As composer John Cage said, *"There is poetry as soon as we realize that we possess nothing"*. The moment is always moving. If we try to harness and control poetry, seeing it as a product of reason, it will elude us. We must quiet our egos to allow words to appear. And as leaders we must let go of our personal desires and agendas - of our unassailability - in order to create voids that others can fill.

Clarity & Simplicity

When we, as leaders, are in danger of being overwhelmed by complex conundrums and competing demands; when others look to us to make complex issues clear and understandable, to cut through the undergrowth of politics and provide balance and insight - we must look to simplicity.

I wouldn't give a fig for the simplicity on this side of complexity; I would give my right arm for the simplicity on the far side of complexity.

Oliver Wendell Holmes

Simplicity is one of the hallmarks of both leadership and poetry; one of the ways meaning is conveyed with elegance and beauty. Simplicity holds our attention. But such simplicity is far from simplistic.

The skillful poet – the careful leader - is able to pare back their words to the moment just before they cease to be clear; to polish a line to an epigram, its meaning sitting delicately. Whether building up or stripping back, the art is in knowing when to stop. Sometimes leading poetically will require us to sit on our hands (and perhaps to close our mouths too). As chinese emperor Han Ling Di argued, we must *"do nothing in order to govern"*.

Leadership Haikus

The haiku is one of the simplest and most compact styles of poetry, classically a three-line poem of 5:7:5 syllables, usually on some theme of nature:

My native village
on approach and to the touch
a bramble rose.

Traditional

I have found haiku writing to be valuable with both individual coaching clients and in vision and strategy work. It can be especially valuable when helping business leaders and solopreneurs to find clarity of purpose. Here are a couple of examples:

Leader hear my heart
hear those other voices, too
clarity will come

Anon

Frail strength; your small voice
Resonates in head and heart;
Leaves fall in Basque dawn.

DM

Length

Long, epic poetry, such as the Mesopotamian *Epic of Gilgamesh* or Dante's omnivorous *The Divine Comedy*, is rare nowadays (although Derek Walcott's highly praised *Omeros* is a notable exception). Instead we tend to see sequences or collections of short poems, whose themes weave around each other like a concept album, such as Philip Gross's *The Water Table*.

Although compact in form (even when not brief) poetry's breadth and scope can be capacious; its impact disproportionate. In today's working environments, attention spans can be short. We need to find ways to engage people quickly, and to hold their attention. We must squeeze the juice out of each interaction.

A poetic approach can help us to engage more effectively in limited time, without making the classic mistake of upping the pace. Ironically when time is short and the stakes are highest, we tend to go into *splurge* mode, trying to get as much information across as possible, as if we have a quota of words we must use up before we lose them. We overwhelm people with dense content and underwhelm them with meaning. Poetry reverses this tendency.

Less is often more. When we pack in the facts (and leave no room for debate) we sound like we are trying to prove a point and may, in fact, protest too much. Too many underdeveloped ideas and undigested facts may provide food for the wrong sort of thought; for picking over the bones of our argument.

Pattern & Sequence

We have already looked at the importance of *repetition* in oratory, the speaker repeating or recasting a point to draw attention to it. Rhetoric also uses devices of *sequence* to achieve particular effects. In English rhetoric for example, we use one for impact, two for comparison, three for wholeness, and four or more to list and expand. The encompassing magic of number three is used in such political tricolons as: "*Never, never and never again*" - Nelson Mandela; "*We cannot dedicate - we cannot consecrate - we cannot hallow*" - Abraham Lincoln; "*Friends, Romans, Countrymen*" - Mark Antony in *Julius Caesar*, by William Shakespeare.

The rule of three also works, for example, in Dante's three line stanzas, which allow for a sense of '*and another thing; and another thing*'.

The Divine Comedy, Canto I

Nel mezzo del cammin di nostra vita
mi ritrovai per una selva oscura
ché la diritta via era smarrita.

translated as:

Midway on our life's journey, I found myself
In dark woods, the right road lost.

The order of things is important in poetry. Sometimes the expected word order is reversed to maintain a particular rhythm or achieve a specific rhyme. The classic word reversal in a chiasmus (such as Keats' *"beauty is truth, truth beauty"* in *Ode on A Grecian Urn*) is a small example of poetic shock.

Most poems have a clear beginning, middle and end, with the sequence of ideas or stanzas being in some logical or chronological order. Sometimes a poet will deliberately change the natural order or flow - put the cart before the horse - to achieve a sense of surprise, or perhaps to play with ideas of cause and effect, or the slipperiness of memory.

Whether deciding on the order of stanzas in a single poem, or of poems in a collection, the poet will *curate* them to create a sense of flow - a naturalness or inevitability (or in some cases the opposite). Our reading of each poem will affect our response to those that follow, the impact   building in stages. The poet may wish us to walk through the rooms of their collection in a particular way (although of course they cannot legislate against us flicking open a book of poetry and climbing in through the bathroom window!).

Much of the real art of leadership is more about this quiet act of curation - of stepping through actions and events in the proper sequence - than it is the staging of operatic spectacle - yet we may pay scant attention to the quotidian choices we make.

Tracing an Arc

The compact form of poetry allows it to traverse a succinct narrative or philosophical arc. A traditional sonnet (or *little song*) usually contains a *volta*, or turn, which contrasts with the unchanging beat of the poem's iambic pentametre. The volta contains either a stress or a flection; a response, or change of mind - or heart. In many sonnets, the first set of lines ask a question or questions, and the remainder answer them.

Grizzly

She-bear on a gravel bar
Rakes swollen salmon from the river,
Broken bodies left to quiver
On the stones with mouths ajar,
Their salmon-urge, the quest to spawn,
Crushed between indifferent jaws.
Sullen, the grizzly overawes—
All must wait till she moves on.

Out of nature draw a symbol—
The claw that rips right through the salmon
Carves the mind to shape an emblem
Of what we fear, and yet resemble.

Keith Holyoak

In some works, the poet brings us back explicitly to their starting point, which we see differently because of the journey we have taken, as T S Eliot suggests:

Little Gidding

We shall not cease from exploration
And the end of all our exploring
Will be to arrive where we started
And know the place for the first time.

Effective leaders trace a narrative arc for us, helping us to see the links in a story, pre-empting doubts and stepping through the parts of their argument, to bring us back to common ground.

The Shape of Your Heart

We have seen how important the shape, form and patterns and sequence of things (words) are in poetry. A poetic leader will pay attention not only to the shape of the things they do, but of the overall shape that their leadership takes; how in their words and deeds, they might embody the kind of leadership they strive for.

13

TELLING THE TRUTH

All truths wait in all things

Walt Whitman

Poetry as Truth

Ralph Waldo Emerson said that the poet writes *"what will and must be spoken"*. The poet's voice can be one of social conscience, and poets are often verbal activists and watchdogs of the truth, in the face of corruption and exploitation. In taking this role, many great poets have carved a courageous, challenging and at times dangerous role for themselves.

Meadowsweet

So they buried her, and turned home,
a drab psalm
hanging about them like haar,
not knowing that the liquid
trickling from her lips
would seek its way down,
and that caught in her slowly
unravelling plait of grey hair
were summer seeds:
meadowsweet, bastard balm,
tokens of honesty, already
beginning their crawl
toward light, so showing her,
when the time came,
how to dig herself out –
to surface and greet them,
mouth young, and full again
of dirt, and spit, and poetry

Kathleen Jamie

Poetry is passion and truth. In an open society, poets speak up and criticise the existing order. Political interference with the ability of poets and other artists to be truthful is often a mark or early warning sign of autocratic control, and the past, ancient and recent, is ripe with tales of killed or exiled writers who have dared to speak the truth.

Poetry has often been an iconic feature of periods of social unrest and revolution, for example in Russia, China, South Africa and Burma. More recently, poetry, including that by Tunisian poet Abu al-Qasim al-Shabi, was a feature of the Arab Spring demonstrations in Tahrir Square.

إذا الشعب يوما أراد الحياة

إذا الشعب يوماً أراد الحيـــــاة	لا بـدّ أن يستجيب القــــدر
ولا بدّ لليل أن ينجلـــــي	لا بـدّ للقيـد أن ينكسـر
ومن لم يُعانـقـه شوق الحياة	تبـخّر في جـوّها واندثـر

The Will to Live

If the people will to live
Providence is destined to favorably respond
And night is destined to fold
And the chains are certain to be broken

And he who has not embraced the love of life
Will evaporate in its atmosphere and disappear.

Abu al-Qasim al-Shabi, translated by As'ad Abu Khalil

Often poems by the dispossessed are about personal, human issues, highlighting a contrast with the impersonal tyranny of the ruling order, rather than being explicitly about oppression.

We see this in Carolyn Forché's short, lyrical poem *The Visitor*, written about El Salvador (which appears in *The Country Between Us*). It has a very different feel to her overtly political prose poem, *The Colonel,* from the same volume.

The Visitor

In Spanish he whispers there is no time left. *
It is the sound of scythes arcing in wheat,
the ache of some field song in Salvador.
The wind along the prison, cautious
as Francisco's hands on the inside, touching
the walls as he walks, it is his wife's breath
slipping into his cell each night while he
imagines his hand to be hers. It is a small country.
There is nothing one man will not do to another.
1979

(this would be *"no hay tiempo que queda"* - no ˈai ˈtjempo ke ˈkeða)

In today's complex organisations, faced with competing demands and a dispersed and disparate workforce, the quest for veracity has never been more vital, nor potentially so tricky.

You are probably familiar with the tale of The Emperor's New Clothes:

A vain and insecure emperor commissions the best attire in the kingdom
from a group of unscrupulous tailors. The tailors hatch a plan, pretending
to make a suit out of the finest cloth in the world - a cloth that only the

incredibly wise can see. Before long all the king's men are madly enamoured with this non-existent suit, and the Emperor is parading naked through his kingdom to rapturous applause. That is, until a young boy steps forward and shouts: "Hey look! The Emperor ain't got no clothes on!"

If we are surrounded by people blandishing us with what they think we want to hear, who can we trust to tell us the truth? Critical friends and honest scrutiny are vital, especially at the top of an organisation. The boards of organisations, for example, should include members who are willing and able to ask the difficult questions.

Another common allegory about where the truth may be heard can be found in stories such as *The Child with the Ears of an Ox* from India and *March's Ears* from Wales. In these stories, a dreadful secret is voiced by a musical instrument, or a plant, as a cypher of truth-carrier. The secret is some animal quality that the protagonist is ashamed of. The voice comes variously from susurrating reeds or whispering bamboo, or from a musical instrument made from a tree or plant. The common message of these allegories is that truth, our essential nature, will out; and maybe that this truth can be found in nature and in music or poetry. A poem is a secret that can't be kept secret any more.

Palimpseas

*Nether Broughton Court, in **the** hamlet of Nether Broughton, which sits on the **wind**ing road between Deddington and Chipping Norton, **remembers the** gracious age of Georgian architecture, **seam**lessly blending eighteenth century grandeur with twenty first century convenience.*

With Chipping Norton (9.5 miles away) it is also in easy reach of the M40 (junctions 10 and 11) providing access to London Heathrow and Birmingham international airports. Train links in the area are particularly good with regular services to London Marylebone from both Bicester and Banbury.

The gardens at Nether Broughton Court enjoy expansive lawns

and yew hedging with terraces and the two attractive "pepper pot"
gazebos. One of two expansive, lawned areas is westerly facing and
reached from the drawing room, the other from the south facing rooms.

A stone built ha-ha separates the formal lawn from the meadow
land beyond, which falls away to the moat. There is a stepped path **that**
can be **used** *in good weather, from the moat* **to** *the two ponds.*

Areas of amenity woodland envelope both sides of the southern
elevation where there are water gardens with additional ponds. The
hard-surfaced tennis court abuts the garden but is protected by the high
stone boundary wall.

The views beyond the moat are of unspoilt **rolling** *countryside,*
*as far away as the top of the Thames Valley, w****here*** *the market town of*
Faringdon nestles in the Vale of the White Horse on the ancient chalk
downlands of Oxfordshire.

Offers in excess of £100,000,000.

Cathy Dreyer

A Language of Truth

The German philosopher Martin Heidegger regarded language as the ultimate
reality, and poetry as the most authentic language. He argued that, in order to
escape the *prison house of language* (the conceptual schemes with which we
organise everything we sense), we need to use language more reverently and
receptively. Heidegger believed poetic language to have a unique capacity to
produce and preserve novelty. His interest was not in the artist or the audience,
but in the 'art' itself, by which he meant know-how, or the means of *bringing
forth*.

Similarly, Coleridge wrote about the skill through which a writer might
*"transfer from our inward nature a human interest and a semblance of truth
sufficient to procure for these shadows of imagination that willing suspension of
disbelief for the moment, which constitutes poetic faith"*; a faith in the, as yet,

unknown that many leaders might give their eye teeth for.

Within the canon, poets have concerned themselves with what it means to write authentically; from both a creative and moral perspective. In her *Notes Towards Authenticity* [33] poet Jane Holland identifies some pointers which have a resonance in the world of leadership, including:

❀ The spirit, rather than the letter, of authenticity is what marks out good poetry. Those who achieve both, or appear to achieve both, are gods.

❀ Rhythm that springs direct from the personality – however contrary and antipoetic - is authentic. Everything else is based on the way we think we ought to be writing.

❀ We cannot steal or borrow or learn authenticity. It's either there in the work or it isn't. Sometimes the only way to find it is to stop looking.

❀ The poet must believe authenticity to be possible, even when faking it like crazy.

It Was Cool Inside The Chapel

It was cool inside the chapel.
Blue torpor had hung over us
for months, cyanising
the pale edge of morning.
Here, even the kids marvelled
at Matisse, adored him.
If you thought anything
of that astonishing patina
cast over white walls
by stained glass in sunlight,
you never communicated it;
turned away, smoking
your ubiquitous cigarette.
Later, we sat contemplating

the blue mosaic of fish
in one of Braque's ceramics.
Nothing had happened.
One person had simply severed
from the other, side by side
in the brilliant aftermath.

Jane Holland

The art of poetry makes important truths accessible and tangible, in contrast with the vague promises made by remote regimes, and disempowering leaders. Here is Scottish poet laureate Kathleen Jamie: *"...if poetry is a method of approaching truths, and each of us with a human soul and 'a tongue in oor heids' can make an approach toward a truth, poetry is inherently democratic."*

So a poetic leader will put truth in the hands of their people, and help them to overcome the nagging sense that people often have (especially in dysfunctional or closed organisations); that someone, somewhere, knows the truth and is not sharing it; that somebody else is *secretly* running the show.

A poem is true if it hangs together.
Information points to something else. A poem points to nothing but itself

E. M. Forster

What is Truth?

Philosophers have debated the meaning of truth for hundreds of years. The ancient Greeks believed that truth was an inherent and static property. Aristotle, for example, defined truth simply as saying *"of what is that it is, and of what is not that it is not"*.

More recent philosophy suggests that truth is a more dynamic property, responding to context and environment. As William James suggested, "Truth happens to an idea. It becomes true, is made true by events. Its verity is in fact an event, a process, the process namely of its verifying itself, its verification." This principle is known as mutability.

Pragmatism judges the truth by its results; by the practical value of its contribution, summarised as *Seeing is Believing*. In contrast, coherence theory calls a thing true when it fits neatly into a well-integrated body of beliefs; summarised as *Believing is Seeing*. We use a balance of both in navigating the world's complexity.

Measure

Linguists and philosophers who describe the criteria for truthful communications often include an aspect of quantity or measure. Grice's Maxims for truthful communications for example, consist of Quantity, Quality, Relation (relevance) and Manner. Similarly, Plato highlighted the importance of *measure* in his dialogue *The Statesman*.

In poetry, brevity is key to aesthetic style and, according to poet Don Paterson, helps a poem to convey its truth: *"if you're using a form of words and not a symbolic mathematical language to express something true about the world, style and brevity are two of the principal means by which those words might more closely approximate that reality."* [12]

Walking the Talk - Embodied Leadership

Embodied leadership is truth in action. We either lead by example or we don't lead at all, our statements and actions being visible reminders to others about what we hold to be important. It is the impact of *who we are being* as we speak and act that leaves the greatest impression on others. People notice if there is a jarring of words and form; we are not seen to be ourselves. (Sometimes of course, both in poetry and leadership, we may use such dissonance to deliberate effect - to draw attention to what is important.)

Walking the Talk also has an impact on the bottom line. Professor Tony Simons found that organisations where managers have *'behavioral integrity'* (where they are seen to follow through on promises and to demonstrate the values they preach) are substantially more profitable than those where they don't. [34]

Leadership As Performance

The concept of leadership as a performing art has been explored by many writers. For example, in *The Arts of Leadership*, Keith Grint describes the conscious enactment or performance of leadership, saying: *"leadership is the world of the performing arts, the theatre of rhetorical skill, of negotiating skills, and of inducing the audience to believe in the world you paint with words and props".*

The performative aspects of leadership involve a repertoire of skills similar to those of an actor: drawing on multiple aspects of self; emotional intelligence; physical enactment (using both voice and body); credibility and presence; and an ability to 'hold' an audience, and an organisation.

So, if we are performing, does that mean we are not telling the truth? According to method acting teacher Sanford Meisner, a good actor is not lying, but *"living truthfully in imaginary circumstances".* We all behave differently under different circumstances. We show different aspects of ourselves to our work colleagues, lover, children and parents. That doesn't mean that we are not being ourselves with each of them. Our dramaturgy is not perceived as false so long as we are authentic.

In their book *Performing leadership*, Peck and Dickinson[35] explore the complex relationship between leadership and performance. Whilst leadership is clearly not a wholly theatrical activity, it is heavily dependent on perceptions. Peck and Dickinson identify the key components of leadership performance as enactment, audience and narrative. They distinguish two types of performance:

❋ *Leadership is performance,* wherein the 'twice performed behaviours' of ritual within organisations (such as committees, presentations and events) literally render leadership a performance. In these rituals, symbols and rhythm are key.

* *Leadership as performance,* based in the context of relationships in organisational life, in which a narrative is enacted and re-iterated in 'once performed behaviours' between leaders and followers. In these relational performances , meaning and connection are paramount.

In order for a leader to be effective, there must be coherence between the two modes; between *ritual* and *relationship*. Leadership is both relational and attributional. Through the leader-follower relationship, people attribute characteristics such as gravitas, authenticity, and integrity to their leaders. We earn the attribution of leadership by our performances. This attribution of leadership in turn shapes our sense of self at least as much as the characteristics of self create the leader. In any leadership performance, the leader herself is both in the moment as a performer and watching the moment, as an observer.

An engaging poem, especially when recited aloud to an audience, will bridge these aspects of ritual and relationship, connecting in the moment even if the poem is one that is often repeated.

Leadership performance is a key area of our work at *Different Development*. We use theatre skills and rehearsal techniques to enable leaders to practice 'doing themselves differently', trying alternative approaches to entrenched problems, and finding an authentic way to be at their best in both ritual and relationship.

The Aesthetics of Truth

Beauty and truth have long been associated. To the ancient Greeks, beauty was not merely a physical quality, but rather some relation of things to our minds, our sense of self and purposes. Classical philosophers argue that beauty is the result of an entity, or an act, adhering to a particular 'form'; one which is harmonious, proportional and pleasing; one which demonstrates the expertise of its maker. Our sense of beauty, whether in a good life, a poem or in leadership, also includes a certain balance and coherence.

Ode on a Grecian Urn

"Beauty is truth, truth beauty," - that is all
Ye know on earth, and all ye need to know.   - Keats

Function is important too. What we perceive as being beautiful in a ballerina will not be beautiful in a wrestler. When we appreciate an object as beautiful, we also recognise the essence of its purpose.

Beautiful leadership therefore incorporates a degree of mastery or craft, a *coherence* between form of expression and overall message, and a sense of purpose. In describing the poetic aspects of leadership, I am also stressing the care and craftsmanship that go into getting it right, and the idea of leadership as *poiesis*; a making of something.

14

SHOWING & TELLING

*If you want to build a ship, don't drum up people together to collect wood
and don't assign them tasks and work, but rather
teach them to long for the endless immensity of the sea*

Antoine de Saint-Exupéry

Show me.....!

"Show, don't tell" is common advice to fiction writers to write in a way that allows the reader to experience a piece through a character's action, words, thoughts and feelings rather than through the narrator's exposition. Instead of being heavy-handed, or overwhelming the reader with adjectives, they should allow the story to emerge from the text; leaving her to draw her own conclusions about what is going on from what she observes and understands.

> *Tell all the Truth but tell it slant---*
> *Success in Cirrcuit lies*
> *Too bright for our infirm Delight*
> *The Truth's superb surprise*
> *As Lightening to the Children eased*
> *With explanation kind*
> *The Truth must dazzle gradually*
> *Or every man be blind---*

Emily Dickinson

Effective writers use detail to breathe life into their writing. Rather than naming emotions (she was afraid; he was angry) they use carefully chosen words alongside appropriate descriptions - stiff, sweaty, a snapped reply, a stammer - to paint a more vivid picture. As Anton Chekhov urged, *"Don't tell me the moon is shining; show me the glint of light on broken glass."*

Arguably, the most *efficient* way of conveying facts to the reader is to tell, and of course there are times when this is the right approach. *Telling* transmits information quickly, and with limited scope for (mis)interpretation; it helps ensure consistent understanding of simple or urgent messages, for example if the building is on fire. But there are often good reasons to take the long way round. *Showing* through the use of action, dialogue, and the five senses, *engages* the reader. It brings information to life and means that the reader doesn't just hear a story, she believes it; she experiences a story as if she was part of it. She empathises with the character and shares in his emotions. She wants to find out what happens next.

Showing is a vital skill for us to cultivate as leaders if we wish to generate dialogue and engage people in co-creation. And in the times when we *do* need shortcuts to get to the crux of the issue (or poem), symbolism, metaphor and other linguistic techniques can play a leading role. Metaphors can somehow hold the most truth in the fewest words. They can get there faster. Whether consciously or not, an engaging leader is likely to be deploying metaphors and other lyrical devices in their communications.

Poetry can be a particularly playful form of showing. A poet often leaves things out; she hints at things, draws parallels. She plays with the reader's imagination. She may write as if she were telling, when she isn't. When Shakespeare' compares Juliet to the sun, he doesn't say Juliet is LIKE the sun, but that she IS the sun.

In *The Love Song of J. Alfred Prufrock*, T. S. Eliot shows us the animal nature of a fog without naming it.

> *The yellow fog that rubs its back upon the window-panes*
> *The yellow smoke that rubs its muzzle on the window-panes*
> *Licked its tongue into the corners of the evening,*
> *Lingered upon the pools that stand in drains,*
> *Let fall upon its back the soot that falls from chimneys,*
> *Slipped by the terrace, made a sudden leap,*
> *And seeing that it was a soft October night,*
> *Curled once about the house, and fell asleep.*

William Stafford's poem *Notice What This Poem Is Not Doing* is also playful, and is unusual in using a showing style of narrative, interspersed with a repeated one line instruction to 'notice' (a telling), that nevertheless avoids the temptation to spell out an answer.

> *The light along the hills in the morning*
> *comes down slowly, naming the trees*
> *white, then coasting the ground for stones to nominate.*
> *Notice what this poem is not doing.*
> *A house, a house, a barn, the old*
> *quarry, where the river shrugs--*
> *how much of this place is yours?*
> *Notice what this poem is not doing.*
> *Every person gone has taken a stone*
> *to hold, and catch the sun. The carving*
> *says, "Not here, but called away."*
> *Notice what this poem is not doing.*
> *The sun, the earth, the sky, all wait.*
> *The crowns and redbirds talk. The light*
> *along the hills has come, has found you.*
> *Notice what this poem has not done.*

William Stafford

Why Showing Works

Why does showing work so much better at engaging people? One reason is that the human brain can be incredibly smug! Most of us love figuring things out for ourselves and often don't like to be *told* (especially that which seems obvious). Many people have dogma antibodies. They want to be given scope to make their own interpretation of the facts (and indeed to stamp their own mark on the way in which they then take action). This may be especially true of individuals with a professional training, or who have particular psychological traits and preferences. People who strongly value intellectual freedom need to be given space to make up their own minds.

There is also evidence to suggest that the harder we have to work to understand something, the more memorable it is. For example, a Princeton study playfully entitled "Fortune favors the **bold** (and the *italicized*)" has shown that readers retain information more reliably when they are challenged with so-called *disfluent* fonts. [36] The more complex a font, the longer our eye lingers on the word, and the longer our brain has to process and retain the information. We also have to work harder. So a communication style that requires people to fill in some of the gaps for themselves will ultimately build commitment. An element of logistic *shock* can have a similar effect.

> *my tears are full of eyes*

from *That Melancholy*, ee cummings

Of course we must maintain a careful balance. We need to cultivate an engaging level of challenge, without straying into the full-blown obtuse which might switch the reader or listener off.

I cannot give the reasons

I cannot give the reasons,
I only sing the tunes:
the sadness of the seasons
the madness of the moons.
I cannot be didactic
or lucid, but I can
be quite obscure and practic-
ally marzipan
In gorgery and gushness
and all that's squishified.
My voice has all the lushness

of what I can't abide
And yet it has a beauty
most proud and terrible
denied to those whose duty
is to be cerebral.
Among the antlered mountains
I make my viscous way
and watch the sepia mountains
throw up their lime-green spray.

Mervyn Peake

Don't Preach

A perpetual challenge for writers and leaders alike - especially when dealing with strong feelings and powerful content (such as difficult organisational challenges and imperatives) - is how to create something moving and engaging that isn't 'preachy'; how to galvanise support without sounding evangelical.

The showing vs telling debate is at the heart of a common problem in contemporary communication. Too many leaders and pundits try to tell us what's going on, rather than showing us. Telling us what's going on is dangerously close to telling us what to think. We see this patronising tendency increasingly in the media, from advertisements to the news, as producers dumb-down and show us picture book images - of ambulances, company headquarters, a generic fireman or a London bus - to illustrate their stories.

Instead, poet Art Durkee encourages us to look for artistic products that move in the direction *"of embodied philosophy, enacted truth, demonstrated-by-example thinking, rather than telling and preaching and pedantry."*

In *Blue Studios* [37] Rachel Blau DuPlessis explores this idea in poetry, comparing poems that try to *think hard for all of us*, and poems that embody thinking as an ongoing, indeterminate process. She describes the difference between: *"Poems that hand you their conclusions on a plate, and poems that encourage you to draw your own conclusions, as a reader. Poems that preach at you, and poems that pull you in by resonating with your own experience."*

Here is some poetic open-mindedness:

WRITING, an excerpt

Plum grainy
veins, unfathomable
noises, moues and wrinkle
winkle

Plumb line, pul-
sing, eye to eye, drinks
dusks of light.

One year after, like a punctuation; one month together, as if
these times had meaning, particular meaning, instead of an
arbitrary path cut through possibly a mistaken hole in the
floor, they thought the radiator was smaller, and there it
is, an unfilled circle ninety years old.

full moon, and hardness   My mother I will, she said.

Rachel Blau DuPlessis

Filling in the Gaps

Showing may also be more satisfying for the leader or artist. Director Anthony Minghella suggested that *"the joy is in giving the audience this fissured, cracked surface, which they then scrub and clean up themselves"*. [38] Each person will produce a slightly different result, that has their own stamp on it; and in doing so, they show that they really *get it*.

Whether, as a leader, you are able to allow this space will depend on circumstances. On whether you simply need to gain consent or ensure a lack of opposition in the moment, or you need genuine and enduring engagement.

Finding the Balance

Of course, neither the skilled poet, or leader, always uses one approach. The balance between *showing* and *telling* is more like a dance. If a writer shows every little thing, the reader may become bored or overwhelmed. Showing makes elements of the writing more vivid, but if it is used   constantly, those parts won't stand out.

And so in work; too much hyperbole, everything equally vivid, and people won't know when something is really important. We need light and shade; focus and relief. As suggested in earlier chapters, we need to vary our tone.

As in a film, 'scenes' that are important to our story need to be dramatised with *showing*, but some of what happens in between scenes can be *told* so the story can make quicker progress. We need to find the right balance of telling versus showing, action versus summarisation, and to bring factors such as rhythm, pace and tone to our aid.

In *This Be The Verse*, Philip Larkin used a combination of humour, rhyme and pace to support him in telling, like it is, a truth that simply had to be told.

A similar balancing act is set out in Hersey and Blanchard's Situational Leadership Model. This model suggests that effective leadership is task-relevant, and that successful leaders adapt their leadership style to the person or group that is being influenced, and the task, job or function that needs to be accomplished. The right leadership style - telling, selling, participating or delegating - will depend on the person or group being led, their 'maturity' as measured by their level of skill, and their willingness to do the particular task.

A leader needs to consciously develop the skills and commitment of their team over time, and shift their style as the team's maturity in this task grows.

The leader's expectations are important too, often becoming self fulfilling prophecies. Conductor Benjamin Zander, co-author of *The Art of Possibility,* tested this phenomenon by awarding his music students top marks at the *start* of their studies. They lived up to his expectations and excelled.

Writers too must assume a level of commitment and capability in their readers and listeners. Even in a short piece of writing, a poet will work to develop interest and understanding. Their use of structure, rhythm, and introduction of certain words, along with tonal and linguistic clues assumes the reader's intelligence and feeds it. This is another aspect of the benign conspiracy between writer and reader; leader and follower.

Humility and the Asking of Questions

In the non-fiction field, and especially in the leadership arena, the avoidance of *telling* has a particular function - the more we are seen to tell people what is so, the less likely many of them are to believe us. The more we explain, the more it can sound like justifying. And the more likely people are to find something to disagree with. In contrast, if we approach our interactions as exploration, with less ego, people will be drawn to us and to our message. In showing, the leader must step back, taking their individual personality and prejudices out of the equation.

The art of showing is closely related to that of asking questions. In showing, we set out a scenario and implicitly ask 'what do you think?'

Effective leaders recognise the power of asking questions. Questions confer power and control to others. It makes them feel listened to, and it allows them a chance to shine. In giving people opportunities to contribute, a leader and their organisation will gain a richer seam of ideas and information to mine, and build a culture in which people are able to think most effectively. The more difficult a situation, or the lower people's level of trust in us, the more critical this balance becomes.

太上，下不知有之；其次，親而譽之；

其次，畏之；其次，侮之。信不足焉

有不信焉。

悠兮其貴言。

功成事遂，百姓皆謂：我自然」。

The best rulers are scarcely known by their subjects;
The next best are loved and praised;
The next are feared;
The next despised:
They have no faith in their people,
And their people become unfaithful to them.

When the best rulers achieve their purpose
Their subjects claim the achievement as their own.

from the ***Tao Te Ching,*** Chapter 17, Lao Tzu

Showing Ourselves

Showing, rather than telling, is also important in a leader's enactment of their own character as a leaders - it is not enough to say 'you can trust me', 'our staff are our most important asset' or 'my door is always open'. People need to see it.

Leaders must touch people on an emotional level, and this requires proof. If we show our people why they should feel enthused, proud or concerned, they will be drawn in. Tell them, and they are likely to demur.

The creation of our own personal 'brand' - or the culture of an organisation;

the perceived role and function of group - is an exercise in showing. We *show* through clear narrative and consistency of voice.

Perhaps above all, people are engaged by real time narratives of growth and change. We best understand the essence of someone by seeing how they respond to events. Showing, then, is closely linked with *becoming*. And again, we are observers of ourselves, as well as actors. When we enact our leadership we are showing ourselves who we are and what we are capable of. This is far more powerful - and believable - than the inner chatter of just telling ourselves.

15

STORY & NARRATIVE

If we hope to live not just from moment to moment,
but in true consciousness of our existence,
then our greatest need and most difficult achievement
is to find meaning in our lives

Bruno Bettelheim

In a fractured age, when cynicism is god, here is a possible heresy: we live by stories,
we also live in them. One way or another we are living the stories that are planted
in us early or along the way, or we are also living the stories we planted --
knowingly or unknowingly -- in ourselves. We live stories that either give our lives
meaning or negate it with meaninglessness. If we change the stories we live by,
quite possibly we change our lives.

Ben Okri

We are Storytelling Animals

A story, narrative or tale is a recounting of a sequence of events, real or imaginary. Storytelling takes place wherever people are, at bedtime, in the newspapers, at the theatre, in an annual report, in the pub, at the family dinner table, or a job interview. At their simplest, stories help us to communicate daily events to each other. They also help us to make sense of the world and our place within it, to create an understanding of our past and to share our hopes for the future.

According to Jungian storyteller Clarissa Pinkola Estes, ancient dissectionists found that the auditory nerve is divided into multiple pathways deep in the brain, and concluded that the ear was meant to hear at three different levels. *"One pathway was said to hear the mundane conversations of the world. A second pathway apprehended learning and art. And the third pathway existed so the soul itself might hear guidance and gain knowledge while here on Earth."* [39]

Why do we love listening to stories? Stories work on an emotional as well as a rational level. A great story will create a limbic resonance in the emotional centre of our brains; a harmony of minds. The limbic activity of those around us can draw our emotions into almost immediate congruence, explaining why *feelings* are contagious, whereas *notions* are not. We might call this kind of connection *love*.

Storytelling has always served an important social function, passing down histories, beliefs and social rules in memorable and emotionally engaging ways. It also has a role in catharsis and the processing of events, especially in difficult times. Oral storytelling is most effective, creating the strongest connection between teller and listener; with a potent element of vocal and physical performance and in-the-moment adjustment to the listener's response.

Great stories tend to share certain features: a protagonist; a familiar predicament; some strange or incongruous element; and strong symbolism. Epic tales often involve movement and sense of direction - perhaps told as a journey though the elements; they take place in imaginative landscapes, where the seasons and mood change; they cover themes of identity and power, of struggle and transformation; there is often some paradox or conundrum.

Common storytelling features, and their significance, have been explored for example in *The Uses of Enchantment* by Bruno Bettelheim and *From The Beast To The Blonde* by Marina Warner.

In *The Hero with a Thousand Faces*, social anthropologist Joseph Campbell describes a *Monomyth*, an archetypal story whose features appear time and again in world mythology. In summary: "*A hero ventures forth from the world of common day into a region of supernatural wonder: fabulous forces are there encountered and a decisive victory is won: the hero comes back from this mysterious adventure with the power to bestow boons on his fellow man.*" [40]

Campbell makes a distinction between the celebrity, seeking self-aggrandisement, and the hero, who acts to redeem society. Celebrity leaders are perhaps all-too familiar. Campbell also likens the path to vocation to the hero's journey, saying that "*We must be willing to let go of the life we planned so as to have the life that is waiting for us.*"

The hero of the monomyth is usually male, which has attracted Campbell some criticism. In contrast, the feminine in traditional stories typically represents creation and ultimate wisdom. Heroine's journeys have also been explored by Maureen Murdock (*The Heroine's Journey*) and Sylvia Brinton Perera (*Descent to the Goddess*).

Stories allow us to explore the subjective experiences of their personae. In traditional stories the characters are often archetypal: the sage, the lover, the wonder child, the magician, the warrior, the queen; and may meet creatures or personified objects along the way. Such stories capture our attention and stimulate the imagination; well-told they will seem eerily familiar, like a premonition, however strange.

Stories, like poetry, can offer us a shorthand; they can 'get deep quick'. Stories are often allegorical, full of symbol; in addition to their surface meaning there is also a more important, deeper meaning. Stories offer us a different kind of truth - one that is disguised or emblematic. We know it in our bones.

Narrative Poetry

Storytelling is an inherent part of much poetry. In traditional narrative poetry, the poet tells a story in verse. A narrative poem has a plot, characters, setting and theme. Narrative poems come in different forms; typically epics such as Homer's *Iliad* and *Odyssey* and the Finish epic The *Kalevala*; romantic idylls such as the medieval French *Romance of the Rose*; lyric poetry (lays), such as that written by Baudelaire and Rossetti; or ballads, such as the traditional *Lord Thomas and Fair Annet*.

Narrative poetry can be comedic or ironic, as for example in Lewis Carroll's tale of *The Walrus and the Carpenter* in *Through the Looking-Glass*.

> The Walrus and the Carpenter
> Were walking close at hand;
> They wept like anything to see
> Such quantities of sand:
> "If this were only cleared away,"
> They said, "it would be grand!"
>
> "If seven maids with seven mops
> Swept it for half a year.
> Do you suppose," the Walrus said,
> "That they could get it clear?"
> "I doubt it," said the Carpenter,
> And shed a bitter tear.

Many other styles of poetry, including much contemporary verse, whilst not traditionally narrative, are biographical (often autobiographical) in nature.

The Leader As Storyteller

The curation and oration of the stories that form the fabric of society, used to be the role of the shamans or elders. Nowadays, in organisations at least, it is that of the leader. Storytelling is seen both as a powerful leadership competency for communication and influencing, and - used diagnostically - as a way to understand and interpret organisational life.

Good leaders have stories even if they don't have all the answers. Stories help us to remember where we have been, and to be clear about who we are and where we are going. Corporate stories are part of the shared history in an organisation. They help to create a sense of connection and belonging; they are social glue. A leader can influence or discern the prevalent zeitgeist by telling or listening to stories. They can create an organisational legacy built on legends that articulate ideas, values and future possibilities.

Moribund organisations tend to lose their stories. Deliberate sharing and repetition of stories will create a ripple effect that helps to maintain the conversational register of an organisation and can help to fill an important gap.

Why Stories Matter

Champions of storytelling argue that they have unique selling points, including that they address neglected areas, such as the impact of people's emotions, values and beliefs on their work, or the tensions between the formal and informal systems at play.

Professor Trish Greenhalgh, Professor of Primary Health Care at University College London, uses stories in qualitative healthcare research. She argues that stories are uniquely able to convey the complexity of human experience in particular contexts and help with paradoxes - problems that can be recognised but not easily resolved. They are therefore of great value in understanding complex and tragic situations. [41]

Stories have much to offer the leader:

❀ Shared and co-created narratives help to underpin sense-making in organisations, generating meaning and engagement around events.

- Stories captivate people's interest and make them more attentive listeners. They communicate information faster, and make it more believable, with more accurate recall of key points over time.

- Storytelling can strengthen relationships, teamwork and trust

- Stories quickly convey the complexity of human experience in particular contexts and so help us to make sense of life within complex systems. They prompt reflection and offer insights into what might have been or could be.

- Stories are often about challenges and 'what best to do'; they help to draw out significant paradoxes - problems that can be recognised but not readily resolved - and foster creative problem-solving.

- Stories have an ethical dimension - coming from our perceptions of the narrative's *particulars* - they inspire the moral imagination

- Stories are performative and action oriented - they ignite action and inspire change. They can connect employees to strategy by providing an understanding of the personal contribution that they can make.

- Stories are non-linear and inherently subversive; they bridge the gap between an organisation's formal and informal space

Narrative approaches enable us to change the frame through which events in an organisation are seen. Over time, these stories become part of the organisation's social fabric. Such stories aren't simply a record of reality, but rather the very stuff that shapes it. Stories don't just point to the gold; they are the gold.

Stories are also an important part of understanding ourselves as leaders. As Barack Obama said, "*I had to know and understand my own story before I could listen to and help other people with theirs*".

Metaphor is an important aspect of story telling. Organisational metaphors and allegories carry disproportionate weight, and will alter people's sense of their work and organisation. Unlike pure facts, they remind people of their similarities rather than differences; the common not the disparate view.

Magic Realism

A great story may feel like magic, but it is no conjuring trick. Storytelling works by directing the audience's attention to what matters - knotting the question to the answer. Effective organisational stories are not about transferring large amounts of information, or transmitting a pre-existing idea. Instead they weave a different cloth by creating novel connections between things the audience already knows, rearranging that information to make new sense of it; to create a fresh idea and a perceptual collage that the audience have co-created. An effective leader gives people a story they can tell themselves.

Extract from *This One Word*
(On Franz Kafka's *The Bucket Rider*)

Winter. Worse than winter.
Kafka shivers, coughs in Berlin
begins a fragment short as breath
about a man who has no coal, hypothermic
and half alive. Phrases halt
at semi-colons, words are cold as rime.
Change of action, change of scene.
Peering into his cellar of thought
the author finds a bucket that flies ...
and we fly too with hope for the man
for treasure itself may be disguised
in a plastic bag or cardboard box and still
be a magical gift.

Mandy Pannett

Of course, not all leadership stories 'land'. We must adapt our approach to the current reality of our audience; if we try to spin a story in a preaching or self-promoting fashion, it may well be viewed as insincere propaganda. The storytelling leader needs to step down from the speech-maker's podium, and create a raw, felt experience that people won't forget.

Colourful stories will be more memorable and enduring than those that are not. Stories need lucid enactment and sensory detail if they are to stick in the mind, and engage our emotions. We need a good balance of familiar anchors and language (to align with the audience) and unfamiliar words and images (to disrupt and challenge their thinking). The electricity of poetic language - of unusual, ambiguous and paradoxical phrases - will grab people's attention.

A sophisticated audience will accept explicit fiction without argument. Questions of accuracy only surface when a thing is said to be literally true. The key questions about an organisational story are 'does it ring true', 'does it makes sense'?

Storytelling has a dark side too and can be ripe with gossip, slander, back-stabbing jokes, cynicism and negativity. These are often part of the narrative undercurrent in organisations, and it may be tempting to echo them as a way of connecting with people. But as leaders we need to be careful with our remit, and conscious of who we are aiming to serve with our stories. As Ben Okri warns, *"A demoralised nation tells demoralised stories to itself. Beware of the storytellers who are not fully conscious of the importance of their gifts, and who are irresponsible in the application of their art: they could unwittingly help along, the psychic destruction of their people"*. [42]

Audience Participation

Stephen Denning, writer of *The Springboard,* describes how listeners to a story are participating in a conceptual journey leading to an unknown mental destination; a place where they can suppose and imagine in order to see the whole picture more clearly. Stories are detailed and specific - deliberate antidotes to the abstract generalities of what *they* or *people round here* always do.

We saw in Chapter 14 how the balance of showing versus telling is important in leadership. As Denning reminds us, it is more effective in the long run to elicit listeners' thinking indirectly; to tell it *slant "with an indirect and ambiguous message, as if whispering in their ears"*. [43]

Incompleteness is inevitable in stories - we can never describe every aspect of a complex narrative - and so listeners will tend to extrapolate, and continue parts of story the way they imagine it should unfold. By trusting our audience to fill in the gaps we can enable them to create their own meaning for a story, resulting in greater personal ownership and a desire to act. Such an audience become the *sponsoring gods* of their stories - their own storytellers. They remain in control and retain their sense of integrity; the co-created story becomes a part of their own evolving sense of identity.

Stories as Diagnostic Tools

Listening to stories is as important for leaders as *telling* them. Leaders who tune in to their organisation's stories will access deeper truths about the values, beliefs, challenges and aspirations of their employees. As Lisa Rossetti suggests, *"In times of pressure and change, stories from colleagues give important information about tacit fears that would not otherwise be discussed."* [44]

Stories and myths evolve naturally out of events in organisations. Yiannis Gabriel argues that the emotions and meanings revealed by organisational stories can tell us a great deal about the 'dreamworld' of the so-called unmanaged organisation - a rich and multidimensional space full of heroes, survivors, victims, lovers and objects of love. [45] Storied accounts offer unique insights into how individuals make sense of their world, and into why people interpret experiences differently.

Polyphonic Stories

Stories evolve as they are being told, by virtue of the teller's current perspective and the listener's input (whether spoken or unspoken). The narratives provide an opportunity for a shift in perception of self and others, for both the teller, and, vicariously, for the listeners too. In effect then, a story is created by two voices in conversation with each other. If the listener's story is unheard, there may be dissonance between these voices. Alternatively, if the story is created collaboratively, a consonant conversation develops.

In *Problems of Dostoevsky's Poetics*,[46] Mikhail Bakhtin describes certain phenomena that are at play in social settings: the unfinalisability of self, the impact of others on self, the polyphonic nature of truth and the role of 'carnival' in creating dialogue. Bakhtin argues that a person is never fully revealed in the world, that they are *"unfinalizable"*, and that every person is influenced by others in an inescapably intertwined way, so that no voice can be said to be isolated. Others will influence the self, not merely in terms of how a person comes to be, but also in how a person thinks and how a person sees him- or herself truthfully.

Bakhtin found in Dostoevsky's work a true representation of *"polyphony"*, each character representing a voice that speaks for an individual self, distinct from others, yet the whole adding up to a polyphonic truth. For Bakhtin, *truth* is a number of mutually addressed, yet inconsistent and contradictory, statements. Truth needs a multitude of voices to carry it. It is part of the leader's role to create the right conditions for this.

Bakhtin also outlined the notion of carnival - the polyphonic context in which distinct individual voices flourish and interact. In Dostoevsky's stories, each character is strongly defined, yet the voices of others are heard by each individual, and each inescapably shapes the character of the other. The carnival creates the *"threshold"* situations where the usual conventions are broken and genuine dialogue becomes possible. Shared storytelling in organisations is one way to create these carnival conditions. A poetic leader will consciously shift the threshold in their organisation, so that genuine dialogue takes place as a matter of course, not just when there is some burning platform.

Organisational Narrative in Schwartz Center Rounds

One example of a conversational space created for stories is the Schwartz Center programme (www.thepointofcarefoundation.org.uk) used in hospitals and other healthcare settings. Schwartz Center Rounds are scheduled multidisciplinary fora for open discussion of the social and emotional issues that arise in caring for patients, with a focus on the human dimension of medicine. Caregivers share their experiences, thoughts and feelings on topics drawn from actual patient cases. Having greater insight into their own responses and feelings helps caregivers to make personal connections with patients and colleagues. According to one participant from an NHS hospital *"There is always hierarchy in a hospital, but in a room like that you are all carers in a caring environment. Your opinion is always listened to."*

Programmes such as this help to create communities of practice. The provision of a forum where people have space and support to say what is so for them, becomes emblematic of the organisation's values. It offers an antidote to the machine or battleground metaphors sometimes used in organisational environments, and a way for people to make sense of events, find meaning in their work, and connect better with others. This is a two-way process - the speaker's truth is witnessed by others. And although their actualities are different, the teller's personal experience resonates with the listener's. A listening forum makes it possible for the speaker to 'overhear' herself say something important. In doing so the truth becomes clearer - and changes - for the listener and the teller too.

Using Narratives

Stories are an important component in our leadership and organisational development work at *Different Development*. Examples include:

- ✺ Helping board members to develop storytelling and deep listening skills;
- ✺ Using narrative techniques to help organisations formulate and embed a meaningful story around their mission, vision and values;

❋ Working with clients' stories to challenge assumptions and default roles or responses, in order to explore different options in a coaching setting;

❋ Using personal narrative poetry writing to explore the balance of factual/non-factual and important/unimportant factors in clients' '*stories*'

❋ Explicitly using mythology and fairytales (including heroes, monsters, beasts and sages) in personal storytelling workshops, helping participants to make sense of their life or career journey, and gain clarity about next steps.

16

FINDING MEANING;
MAKING SENSE

While science may lead you to truth, only imagination can lead you to meaning.

C. S. Lewis

Charting the Territory

One of the most important tasks of today's leaders, especially in times of uncertainty and change, is to help people make sense of things. A good leader is able to help others find meaning, by providing context and by helping people find a sense of what they do and where they fit. They give voice to passion and personality in the workplace, by living their vocation, and so help others to find theirs. Leaders frame the issues in a way that people can respond to positively.

Expressing our feelings in words, or sometimes even identifying them, can be difficult, especially when we are feeling uncertain or alone. As leaders we may often find ourselves in uncharted territories, relying on our intuition. Yet we are called upon not only to make sense of this place for ourselves, but to plant meaning in other people's hearts. In a complex environment, where there are no longer jobs for life, and external demands can change rapidly, people may struggle to make sense of the business they work in, and particularly of their own role within it. People are looking to their leaders to provide an authentic narrative about work and business.

We need to transmit meaning, but we work with people who have divergent views and perspectives; who are motivated by unlike things, and may hold dear, values that are alien to us. We need to find somewhere for different values and beliefs to meet, and a language that helps to build and share meaning.

The language of poetry can guide us. Poets help us to define what it is to be human. They speak, implicitly or explicitly, of soul and spirit. They help us to find our place in the world, and in respect to other people in it. Poetry explores the unknown, raises questions and seeks meaning.

As Robert Frost suggests, a poem is *"a clarification of life—not necessarily a great clarification such as sects and cults are founded on, but in a momentary stay against confusion."* [47]

Poetry also spans the divide between the intellectual and the emotional; the known and the felt. Holding its content lightly, poetry is able to communicate both an *idea* and the *feeling* associated with that idea - the two entwined - with clarity and precision. In most organisational challenges, the interface between the rational and the emotional is the place where the leadership quest succeeds or fails.

Using symbol, metaphor and other linguistic devices, poetry can weave a coverlet of thoughts, feelings and concepts that might elude the more literal language of prose. It helps us make sense of confusing observations and chaotic experiences.

Sitting at the interface of reason and 'rhyme', poetry defies our natural resistance to dogma. It comes at us at a tangent, from our peripheral vision, and lodges in our hearts and minds. Poetic devices such as metaphor, can engage and clarify, whilst leaving room for individual interpretation. They emphasise similarity, yet are tolerant of difference. Using a poetic mindset, a leader can make meaning of their aspirations, and inspire others to action.

Framing reality

Max De Pree suggests that leaders have the responsibility of defining reality. Leaders help us to see things more clearly, sometimes by going beyond the superficial; by looking through a different lens. Effective leaders can draw a different frame around the same set of circumstances, resulting in an alternative perspective, and new options.

Poetry plays a similar role. George Santayana suggests that its function is "*to seize hold of the reality of sensation and fancy beneath the surface of conventional ideas;... to build new structures.. fitter to the primary tendencies of our nature, truer to the ultimate possibilities of the soul.*" [48]

If we can convey some of this deeper reality to people, we will more vividly engage their senses and enlist their support. Poets pay attention to detail, and get to the true heart of reality and experience.

Our frames of reference, or mental models, are deeply ingrained images, assumptions and generalisations, that influence how we understand the world and how we act. These models affect our behaviour, and because we tend not to be aware of the frame, we don't realise that we disregard information that doesn't fit our reality. It is useful to turn the mirror inward; to expose our internal pictures of the world to scrutiny.

William Blake who, as an engraver, was familiar with the revelatory powers of acid on metal, suggested that *"poetry cleanses the doors of perception"*. Poetry can help us to make a distinction between *presented* and *represented* realities, and therefore to develop the skills to reframe information for ourselves and others.

> *I dwell in Possibility --*
> *A fairer House than Prose --*
> *More numerous of Windows --*
> *Superior -- for Doors --*
> *Of Chambers as the Cedars --*
> *Impregnable of Eye --*
> *And for an Everlasting Roof*
> *The Gambrels of the Sky --*
> *Of Visitors -- the fairest --*
> *For Occupation -- This --*
> *The spreading wide of narrow Hands*
> *To gather Paradise --*

Emily Dickinson

Sensemaking

It was organisational theorist Karl Weick who popularised the idea that certain phenomena, including the abstract idea of an 'organisation', are created by being talked and written about. He said: *"Managers construct, rearrange, single out, and demolish many 'objective' features of their surroundings. When people act they unrandomize variables, insert vestiges of orderliness, and literally create their own constraints".*[49] In his work on sensemaking in organisations, Weick echoes E. M. Forster, saying *"How can we know what we think until we hear what we say?".*

Rather than poetic leaders believing that they have all the answers, they find out what is important through reflection and engagement. They might develop the seed of a vision or an idea in dialogue with others, much as a writer will use the act of writing to gain understanding, thought shaping the shaper.

Writer Art Durkee describes this creative process: *"People who have something to say are propagandists, advertisers, marketers, and zealots. What they have to say is the most important thing, to them. Writers, on the other hand, very often don't know what they have to say, until they say it. And maybe not always then".*

We might imagine this process playing out as poet Elizabeth Bishop explores her reactions, as if for the first time, as she writes her villanelle, One Art; the losses more and more significant as the poem progresses to its close:

> *-- Even losing you (the joking voice, a gesture*
> *I love) I shan't have lied. It's evident*
> *the art of losing's not too hard to master*
> *though it may look like (Write it!) a disaster.*

> Elizabeth Bishop

A Meaning in Motion

A poem contains movement in time and space; an unfolding of dramatic events. As critic and dramatist Gotthold Ephraim Lessing describes in *The Laocoon*, whilst painting observes spatial proximity, and therefore, has to represent the defining moment in a series of events, poetry depicts an event as it evolves in time. *"The essence of poetry thus lies not in description but in the representation of the transitory, of movement."* [50] Poetry embodies change; it cycles and breathes - now this, now this, now this. Its meaning is not fixed. Its unfolding leaves time for us take on board each new theme. And it is likely to unfold differently each time we read it.

> *Now wind has died in the lime trees*
> *I have forgotten what sense they made,*
> *but not the leaf the wind dislodged*
> *that fell between my shoulder blades.*

Extract from *Fall*, Andrew Motion

Making Words Work Harder

Words can have many meanings, both literal and symbolic, as studied in the disciplines of semantics and pragmatics. We can learn much about these approaches from the great teacher, Humpty Dumpty, who discusses them with Alice in Lewis Carroll's *Through the Looking Glass*.

"When I use a word," Humpty Dumpty said in a rather a scornful tone, "it means just what I choose it to mean -- neither more nor less."
"The question is," said Alice, "whether you can make words mean different things."
"The question is," said Humpty Dumpty, "which is to be master -- that's all."

Humpty Dumpty claims to be able to use words, like "glory" and "impenetrability", to mean just what he wants them to mean, neither more nor less. But when he makes a word work harder, carrying an added layer of idiosyncratic meaning, he "pays it extra". Poets too give words multiple meanings, making the words and their readers work.

In *Betweenland VI* from *The Water Table*, Philip Gross gives us two kinds of gulls. The birds "*going home from the city*", and the gull or bamboozling of a homophone in "*even the Vikings/ left just the hull of a word: Holm./ Make of that sound what you will.*"

Such wordplay is very different to the woolly or lazy use of vocabulary we sometimes see in management speak, such as 'taking it offline' or 'to the next level', 'deliverables', 'incentivise' and the quasi-verb 'to project-manage'.

We use words to mean what we want them to mean. Usually we're careful to use them in ways that other people immediately understand. But sometimes we can make a word work *extra hard* by giving it freedom, allowing it to speak volumes, enrich ideas, celebrate possibilities, spark ideas; by letting it resonate and perhaps suggest meanings we hadn't even thought of. Like Humpty Dumpty, poets use words in magical ways to trick our brains into life.

The Shock of Poetry

A very specific example of stimulating the brain through unusual word use occurs in a feature of the English language known as *anthimeria* or functional shift. In this, new words are created by changing the part of speech (class) of existing words, for example using a noun or an adjective, to serve as a verb. The language is *weirded*. Functional shift is commonly associated with Shakespeare, who used it to vivid dramatic effect, for example in the phrase '*I could out-tongue your griefs*'. Functional shift changes the grammatical nature of a word with little change to its shape, and is colloquially referred to as '*nerbs and vouns*'.

Such sudden changes of shape catch the brain off guard and create a sense of drama, as language moves fluidly from one sense to another in a mental flash. Phil Davis and Neil Roberts, of Liverpool University, and Guillaume Thierry of Bangor University, looked at what happens in the brain in the momentary hesitation that occurs when we read an example of functional shift.[51] The result matches a brain wave (EEG) phenomenon that usually occurs when we read a grammatically incorrect sentence, but with none of the effects normally associated with reading a text that does not make semantic sense. In other words, we accept the meaning of the word first, and then go on to re-evaluate how it makes sense. There is a peak in brain activity whilst the brain works backwards to understand what Shakespeare is trying to say. This lightning-fast effect is often experienced in poetry and is perhaps why great poetry is said to communicate before it is understood.

Making our brains work extra hard may be one reason that Shakespeare's plays have such a dramatic impact. Any linguistic technique that stimulates our brains, whilst holding our attention, can be hugely powerful, and can render the content more moving and more memorable.

Snow

The room was suddenly rich and the great bay-window was
Spawning snow and pink roses against it
Soundlessly collateral and incompatible:
World is suddener than we fancy it.

World is crazier and more of it than we think,
Incorrigibly plural. I peel and portion
A tangerine and spit the pips and feel
The drunkenness of things being various.

And the fire flames with a bubbling sound for world
Is more spiteful and gay than one supposes -
On the tongue on the eyes on the ears in the palms of one's hands -
There is more than glass between the snow and the huge roses.

Louis Macneice

Complexity & Imperfection

The reality of the working environment is one of imperfection, uncertainty and sometimes chaos. We may be seduced into developing an armoury of conviction and fixity in our defence. And yet there may be a deeper resilience to be found in an acceptance of the beautiful truth.

One of the humanising characteristics of great art of any kind is often that it is subtly flawed; a portrait that is not photo-perfect yet tells us infinitely more about the sitter; a handwoven shawl that is slubby and uneven; a line of poetry that is pared back and degraded, until its meaning is precariously fragile.

In *Poetry and the Rhetoric of Management*,[52] Jim March of Stanford University suggests that intelligent comprehension needs to be protected from the *"simplifying necessities of managerial life"*, and argues that poetry and metaphor can help with this. *"Poetry is a voice of an incoherent truth. It reminds managers and their advisors that life is gloriously chaotic and endlessly confusing, that contradictions of feelings and comprehensions bring a bittersweet, but essential, enrichment to life...."*

Poet A. R. Ammons agrees that poetry can offer a mental reprieve, and protection against over simplification: *"Poetry leads us to the unstructured sources of our beings, to the unknown, and returns us to our rational, structured selves refreshed. Having once experienced the mystery, plenitude, contradiction, and composure of a work of art, we afterward have a built-in resistance to the slogans and propaganda of oversimplification that have often contributed to the destruction of human life.."* [53]

Extract from *Easter 1916*

Too long a sacrifice
Can make a stone of the heart.

W. B. Yeats

17

THINKING & LEARNING

I have no axe to grind; only my thoughts to burnish.

George Santayana

Introduction

One of the most important qualities identified by champions of poetry for the workplace is its power to develop new thinking skills; skills that emphasise wisdom and learning over knowledge, creative over fixed ideas.

Why is this so important in today's organisations? Leaders are the midwives and guardians of organisational thinking and learning. We increasingly live in an age where knowledge, especially the kind of knowledge that is intangible and complex, is one of our most valuable commodities.

Leaders need to be able to think creatively and realistically. They need to understand the details yet see the big picture. They are likely to be curious for discovery, and to see possibility in things, sharing their thinking and learning unselfishly. Leadership means not only being informed but becoming wiser and better at learning.

The Poetic Mindset

A traditional perspective of the mind suggests that thought and language are inherently literal and that poetry (with its highly figurative nature) requires special cognitive and linguistic skills. In *Poetics of Mind,* [54] Ray Gibbs shows how figurative aspects of everyday language reveal the deeply poetic nature of mind. He argues that our figurative imagination determines the way we understand ourselves and the world in which we live. If true, then we should surely acknowledge the poetic nature of the human mind in that complex human arena, the world of work.

In his essay *Science and Poetry,* I. A. Richards describes the experience of reading poetry *from the surface inwards,* from the impression of the printed words on the retina, to the sound of the words *in the ear* and the feel of the words imaginarily spoken, to pictures *in the mind's eye* of things for which the words stand, thence to two streams of experience - the minor intellectual stream, and the major one of "*the play of our interests*" - our emotions and attitudes. Richards suggests that the latter is paramount: "*Our thoughts are the* servants of our interests, and even when they seem to rebel it is usually our interests that are in disorder. Our thoughts are pointers and it is the other, the active, stream which deals with the things which thoughts reflect or point to."

Thinking & Knowing

In spite of diversifying into genres, such as rap and slam, that attract a broad audience, poetry is traditionally seen as an intellectual or elitist pursuit, and for some this is an unattractive association. Poet Don Paterson is unapologetic about it, reputedly saying *"Read poetry: it's quite hard"*. Perhaps it is poetry's very seriousness that sees it threatened in a culture of consumerism; where ignorance becomes something to be proud of and products all start to look the same.

The developed world's approach to knowledge over the last century has been to reduce it to analytic propositions. Yet a *Napoleonic* approach to scientific enquiry can result in rules, myopia and stagnation. Moreover, as Complexity and Completeness Theories tell us, science and mathematics are not enough.

*Extract from **Love***

The book of Sufi wisdom
Is not written on the blank page,
But on a heart white as virgin snow.
Scholars pursue penmarks.
Sufis track footprints in the snow,
Like hunters tracing a musk – deer's trail,
Until they breathe in the sweet scent
That the deer exudes from its navel,
And rush to catch their quarry.

Rumi

In a world of rapid change where innovation and flexibility are key to success, we need a more Tolstoyan approach built on *creative anarchy*. Poetry's focus on ideas over facts can help us not only to create a shared understanding, but to guard against unhelpful certitudes.

Rational thinkers look for the truth in the supposed certainty of scientific, legal, scholarly, or technical jargon. They perhaps, like Socrates, underestimate the veracity and precision of poetic language. Poets and other artists, on the other hand, see the limitations of language; they see things which cannot easily be described in words. Some, such as Steven Spender, [55] also mistrust an excess of knowledge: *"For there are examples enough to show... that the poetic imagination is harmed by absorbing more intellectual knowledge than it can digest"*.

In Voltaire's Bastards,[56] John Ralton Saul argues against society's fixation with rational solutions:

> *Reason is a narrow system*
> *swollen into an ideology.*
>
> *With time and power it has*
> *become a dogma, devoid of*
> *direction and disguised as disinterested inquiry.*
>
> *Like most religions, reason*
> *presents itself as the solution*
> *to the problems it has created.*

Saul seeks to rescue reason from the bureaucrats he believes have claimed it, given it preeminence, and reduced it to pure administration.

Jerome Bruner describes two kinds of knowing In *On Knowing: Essays for the Left Hand*. [57] The objective, order and lawfulness, *le droit* (right handed) and the subjective, expressive hypotheses and dreams (left handed). He argues that, in our quest for knowledge, we tend to reach with the right hand, and leave the way of the left unexplored: *"a way that grows happy hunches and 'lucky' guesses, that is stirred into connective activity by the poet and the necromancer looking sidewise rather than directly. Their hunches and intuitions generate a grammar of their own - searching out connections, suggesting similarities, weaving ideas loosely in a trial web."*

Of all modes of human language - of expression of thought - poetry brings together the subjective and objective parts of the thinking process most tangibly. The rational and non-rational aspects of our mental processes tend to be concentrated in the left and right hemispheres of the brain respectively (in a right handed person). We can see the impact of losing either function when brain damage occurs. For example, as neuroanatomist Jill Bolte Taylor describes in her memoir, *My Stroke of Insight*. [58] A stroke in Taylor's left brain temporarily shut down a large part of her rational functioning, allowing more of her right brain function to surface. Right brain thinking includes emotions and intuition, conceptualisation, linking of patterns and random thoughts, and in Taylor's experience, an uncanny sense of bliss.

The neural connections between the left and right hemispheres pass through the *corpus callosum*, a structure in the centre of the brain associated with the most elaborate mental activities, including the integrated use of verbal and visuo-spatial thought that is necessary for many types of creative thinking, and heavily employed in both writing and reading poetry.

He is quick, thinking in clear images;
I am slow, thinking in broken images.
He becomes dull, trusting to his clear images;
I become sharp, mistrusting my broken images,

From *In Broken Images*, Robert Graves

Wisdom

Wisdom (as opposed to knowledge) is a quality that shows up in action; in our behaviours. The people we describe as wise do not necessarily know a lot of things, but they are able to swiftly and elegantly apply what they do know. This goes beyond mere cleverness, as a great poem uses language to get beyond language.

Wisdom lies not in having fixed ideas, but in modifying our perspective in the light of experience and, sometimes, criticism. It is perhaps better thought of as an ongoing process, a *coming-to* rather than a fixed resource that can be kept safe. Wisdom requires humility.

Wisdom is open-minded. As Peter Drucker asserts, a common source of mistakes in management is an emphasis on finding the right answer rather than the right question.

We can develop non-linear thinking skills and a deeper resilience to change and uncertainty, using approaches that enable us to pause and reflect. Clutterbuck and Megginson for example, argue that coaching and mentoring can be of value in this context, helping us to develop the creativity, self awareness and emotional intelligence that are key to resilience.

A leader's wisdom crucially includes a finely-tuned awareness of what is going on around them. This usually involves intuition and processes in the subconscious mind. It doesn't mean that some magical power is at work; rather that effective leaders develop a deep appreciation of their situation and surroundings.

Flexibility

In 1964, anthropologist Thomas Gladwin recounted the different navigational tactics used by western European and native *Trukese* sailors, which illustrate deterministic versus emergent styles of thinking.[59]

The European navigator uses a sequential plan or course for their journey. The plan consists of directions, degrees of longitude and latitude, and estimated times of arrival at each point on the journey. The plan can be recited if needed. This logical approach works well in predictable conditions. However, should circumstances change, the 'left-brained' sailor must first adjust the plan, before continuing to follow its steps.

In contrast, the *Trukese* sailor starts by imagining the position of his destination relative to other landmarks. He sets off and adjusts direction *ad hoc* as he sails, keeping aware of the elements and his relative position and destination. His approach to navigation is fluid, improvised and difficult to put into words. Yet the *Trukese* sailor can adapt on-the-move if the unexpected happens.

For many people, and in most organisations today, life is complex and unpredictable, and requires flexibility. This is one of the most common challenges that clients bring to my leadership coaching. *"It's chaos. Everything is so up-in-the-air at the moment. But it will be better once things are settled"* is a familiar cry.

A capacity to remain open and flexible, suspending immediate judgements, is a real leadership strength. Skilled leaders can approach situations from a variety of angles and generate a range of possibilities for action. Less effective managers may be seduced into tackling problems with a rigid approach, and can get stuck when they come up against barriers they cannot get around.

The kind of wisdom or knowledge that is useful to us may be difficult to get from the traditional classroom or report. Perhaps it is not to be found in what passes for *the new*.

From *Asphodel, that greeny flower*

My heart rouses
                    thinking to bring you news
                                of something
        that concerns you
                    and concerns many men. Look at

what passes for the new.

You will not find it there but in
despised poems.

It is difficult
to get the news from poems
yet men die miserably every day
for lack
of what is found there.

Hear me out
for I too am concerned
and every man
who wants to die at peace in his bed
besides.

William Carlos Williams

How Poetry Helps Us Think

Greater exposure to reading or studying poetry can have a number of benefits, but a key one seems to be the way it enhances certain thinking skills. In *What Poetry Brings to Business*, Clare Morgan explores the impact on individuals of reading poetry, and argues a role for poetry in developing different, more strategic, thinking.

According to Morgan, "*Reading poetry generates conceptual spaces that may be different from the spaces usually available to (business) strategists*". She suggests that these spaces are associative rather than causal; are imaginative rather than deductive; offer new ways of assessing relations between things; and encourage a radical scepticism about the nature of 'fact'.

Poetry uses relatively unpredictable language and surprising imagery; it arrests the ear and the mind with novelty, patterns, powerful metre and fresh ideas; it requires us to remain alert and pay attention. By doing all this, poetry reduces what is known as 'automatic perception' and helps us to question our assumptions. To read poetry requires us to claim that imaginative space, to live with uncertainty, rather than rush to conclude and summarise.

As Viktor Shklovsky writes: *"we find material obviously created to remove the automatism of perception; the author's purpose is to create the vision which results from that deautomatized perception."* [60]   This makes objects unfamiliar, and prolongs the process of perception, as an aesthetic end in itself, making poetic language and its subject matter appear strange and wonderful.

A Fixed Idea

What torture lurks within a single thought
When grown too constant; and however kind,
However welcome still, the weary mind
Aches with its presence. Dull remembrance taught
Remembers on unceasingly; unsought
The old delight is with us but to find
That all recurring joy is pain refined,
Become a habit, and we struggle, caught.
You lie upon my heart as on a nest,
Folded in peace, for you can never know
How crushed I am with having you at rest
Heavy upon my life. I love you so
You bind my freedom from its rightful quest.
In mercy lift your drooping wings and go.

Amy Lowell

Thinking Differently

Leaders must be able to balance seemingly conflicting priorities - the needs of customers, staff and share-holders or tax-payers. To be effective, they need appositional thinking skills; to consider juxtapositions and arrive at a deep integration of seemingly contradictory concerns. They will also need to apply a different mindset at different times: reflective, analytic, strategic, collaborative and action mindsets all have their role.

As Einstein told us, *"We can't solve problems by using the same kind of thinking we used when we created them."* When we are stuck, we may need to try a different thinking approach. Traditional management approaches tend to follow inductive or deductive logic, suggesting: *"If you can't measure it, you can't manage it"*. Whilst this enables us to extrapolate from the known facts and from past experience, it is of limited value when we are trying to anticipate the unknown consequences of a reality that has yet to be. We can't create something that we can't imagine. Poetry's abductive thinking style may help us to develop the necessary skills.

Decisions & Questions

Effective leaders are able to make *good* decisions - although not necessarily singular, *right* decisions - even when the facts before them are slippery or sparse.

Good decision making has an important emotional component, as Antonio Damasio argues in *Descartes's Error.* [61] He suggest that Descartes was wrong to assert the dualism of mind and body, and that our bodies and emotions are as important in thinking as our rational brains are. In other words our mind is embodied, not just embrained. Damasio describes studies showing that decision making is impaired in people who have suffered damage to the emotional centres in the upper right hemisphere of the brain.

Questions are vital too. One of the most effective shifts I have found with coaching clients, is helping them to prioritise questions over statements in their interactions with others. This is valuable not only for the rich seam of new information that opens up to them, but also for the important and empowering message that it sends to their teams.

I think that poetry encourages us to consider a richer range of questions. It shows us different points of view; it enables us to make complex comparisons; it focuses us above all on the question "what does it mean?".

Sharpening Our Skills

Just as ethical knowledge comes from our perceptions of the particular not the general, so literature has the power to develop not only our imaginations, but our ethical awareness. We become better at imagining the position of others as the sentiments we are introduced to become, in some measure, our own.

Martha Nussbaum for example argues that *"literature is an extension of life not only horizontally, bringing the reader into contact with events or locations or persons or problems he or she has not otherwise met, but also, so to speak, vertically, giving the reader experience that is deeper, sharper, and more precise than much of what takes place in life."* [62]

Horizontal and vertical links are created not only between our experience and the imaged experience of others, but between different realms of life, and different modes of thinking.

Art is vitally about using cross modal links to stimulate our hearts and minds. Poetry specifically is a verbal means to nonverbal images; images which manifest emotional expression. All art forms can help to develop our cross modal sensing and thinking skills. They utilise allegory, metaphor and abstract thinking; they connect our auditory, visual and kinaesthetic experiences. (Interestingly, the sweet touch of synaesthesia is far more common in artists than in the general population.) The creation of horizontal links between experiences, issues or thinking modes, serves to deepen our view of the particular, and this greater depth sparks, in turn, new associations - new horizontal links.

A Learner & a Teacher

People who are able to wrest meaning from experience are successful. They can apply learning in one area of their life to others, using cross application of experiences. They are not just learning, but learning *how to learn*, and learning better. They demonstrate learning agility.

And it is not enough for the leader alone to have the answers; to do all the thinking and learning. True leaders are teachers too. They build environments in which people can reflect and learn, solve problems and learn self-leadership. They teach others how to learn, and in turn to respect and develop others.

Like well crafted poems, the poetic leader won't tell us what to think, or do our thinking for us, but they might be able to teach us something about how to.

Creating a place where people can do their best thinking is the focus of Nancy Kline's work on *Thinking Environments*, detailed in her book *Time To Think*. Leaders can help to create an environment where others communicate in a clear, open and straightforward way, above all by listening and paying attention. Listening in a thinking environment is a generative process.

Here is a haiku written by Nancy in a workshop I ran on Poetry in Coaching in 2012:

> *I listen to you*
> *You break through. No words from me.*
> *Act of Creation*

In any organisation or group, thought is largely a collective phenomenon, occurring in *dialogue*. As quantum physicist David Bohm argues, effective thinking requires us to become open to the flow of a larger intelligence. [63] Bohm also stresses that the thinking process (like a map) "*is a representation of what is, but is not what is*". Poetry (like any explicit fiction or other-person narrative) helps us to distinguish between presented and represented realities, and to be more acutely aware of a range of alternative interpretations and meanings we could ascribe to the same Newtonian *facts*.

Ambiguity

While of course facts are important, they are not enough. Lominger International's research on '*The leadership skills that matter*', suggests that the most important competency in short supply today is dealing with ambiguity. [64] People who are tolerant of ambiguities cope relatively well where information is vague, incomplete or inconsistent, and where the solution and means of getting there are not immediately clear. Supple thinkers, they are comfortable with open-ended or ambiguous problems and tend to enjoy the autonomy that loosely-defined tasks require. Such flexibility and dynamism is key to creative performance. Tolerance of ambiguity is also associated with particular psychological types, for example those who are 'perceivers' rather than 'judgers' on the Myers-Briggs MBTI scale, or 'sharpeners' in Gestalt thinking.

Gestalt Psychology identifies two sets of preferences, or cognitive strategies, around perception. Levellers are anxious to categorise sensations and less willing to give up a category once established. They level or suppresses differences and emphasises similarities in the interest of perceptual stability. In contrast, sharpeners tolerate unclassifiable sensations, and may actually seek out ambiguity. They are able to keep in mind various aspects of a given whole, to plan conceptually, and to think and act symbolically.

Poetry, and the poetic leader, are inherently 'sharpener' in nature. Moreover, literary theorist Reuven Tsur [65] has shown that literary training develops our 'sharpener' skills, equipping us to detect subtle nuances.

Curious exploration, and a willingness to sit with unresolved questions, mirror the creative structure of poetry rather than the concrete answers of prose. Keats called this tolerance 'negative capability': "*that is, when a man is capable of being in uncertainties, mysteries, doubts, without any irritable reaching after fact and reason*".[66] We grow by sitting with the questions rather than knowing all the answers; by befriending the unknown.

Poetry is a country of no right answers; a land of light and shade, of paths that may lead somewhere or nowhere; a territory of lookout points and places to rest.

Knowledge

My philosopher friend is explaining again
that the bottle of well-chilled beer in my hand

might not be a bottle of beer,
that the trickle of bottle-sweat cooling in my palm

might not be wet, might not be cool,
that in fact it's impossible ever to know

if I'm holding a bottle at all.
I try to follow his logic, flipping the steaks

that are almost certainly hissing
over the bed of coals – coals I'd swear

were black at first, then gray, then red –
coals we could spread out and walk on

and why not, I ask, since we'll never be sure
if our feet burn, if our soles

blister and peel, if our faithlessness
is any better or worse a tool

than the firewalker's can-do extreme.
Exactly, he smiles. Behind the fence

the moon rises, or seems to.
Have another. Whatever else is true,

the coals feel hotter than ever
as the darkness begins to do

what darkness does. Another what? I ask.

Philip Memmer

18

SUSTAINING CREATIVITY

I have lived on the lip
of insanity, wanting to know reasons,
knocking on a door. It opens.
I've been knocking from the inside.

Rumi, from *The Turn*

The New Black

Why is creativity thought to be so important in the workplace today? Several recent studies have identified complexity and uncertainty as the biggest challenges facing CEOs today. Based on conversations with over 1500 CEOs across all sectors worldwide, IBM's 2010 Global CEO Study identifies creativity as *"the single most important leadership competency for enterprises seeking a path through this complexity."* [67]

Creative leaders are thought to innovate more. They have novel ideas. They create new products. They come up with different ways to get things done. Just as artists have tools that enable them to move from intention to creation and expression, so we can develop similar approaches in leadership. Poetry has a grammar of possibility, and reading poetry can help to develop (amongst other things) creative thinking skills and tolerance of ambiguity. These are vital skills in today's complex world.

Change is the biggest challenge, and the most flexible component in any system is the human being. Forward thinking Chairs and Chief Executives say they want creative organisations; people with new mind sets, whose flexible thinking enables them to overcome obstacles. Yet people can be wary of some of the means of facilitating creativity. Capabilities drawn from the creative arts can bring new insights, some specific and tangible, others less so.

In his book *A Whole New Mind* [68] Daniel Pink describes a new *Conceptual* age of work, and argues that the future of global business belongs to the right-brainer, with creativity and empathy being the key competitive differences. Pink outlines six senses essential in this new environment: Design - moving beyond function; Story - moving beyond argument; Symphony - adding invention and the big picture; Empathy - going beyond logic to engage emotion and intuition; Play - bringing humour and light-heartedness to business; and Meaning - the purpose is the journey, give meaning to life from inside yourself. There are echoes of these senses in the chapters of this book.

Dr. Amantha Imber [69] has also identified the top predictors of creative performance in the workplace. These include ideas that are key in poetic thinking, such as intuition, tolerance of ambiguity and cross application of experiences. Poetic thinking is expansive and open-ended; it is focused on conceptualisation above facts. Poetry's appositional thinking - the art of uniting opposites in interesting and memorable ways - lies at the heart of creativity.

Imagination is more important than knowledge.
For knowledge is limited to all we now know and understand,
while imagination embraces the entire world,
and all there ever will be to know and understand.

Albert Einstein

Innovation & Improvisation

Effective leaders work at the edge of their ability; they may well make mistakes, but they are able to learn from them and move on. They are working at a moving edge; a place of not knowing, of adventure and creativity, where current knowledge asymptotes to nothing.

This place of the unknown is encountered in many fields. The physicist Niels Bohr observed that, '*When it comes to atoms, language can be used only as in poetry. The poet, too, is not nearly so concerned with describing facts as with creating images and establishing mental connections*'. [70]

Only by reaching a place of not knowing can we discover the new. Scientists and leaders in this hinterland work with existing knowledge, intuition and perhaps a little magic. They become *poets*, assuming an attitude towards the merely possible, and imagine (or write) something new into being. This is their *auth*ority.

Stephen Spender described poetic invention as beginning with: "*a dim cloud of an idea which I feel must be condensed into a shower of words*". [71] Such an idea may be elusive and must be held lightly.

Leadership is often improvisational and spontaneous. We have to carve out new paths with whatever resources we have - our current understanding, people and skills and other resources. Like an actor on stage, we may wish that we had a different set, props or supporting cast; but we have to create magic with whatever we have, and from whoever we are. We have to improvise.

In *Composing a Life*, Mary Catherine Bateson suggests that *"Improvisation can be either a last resort or an established way of evoking creativity."* adding *"I believe that our aesthetic sense, whether in works of art or in lives, has over-focussed on the stubborn struggle toward a single goal rather than on the fluid, the protean, the improvisatory."* [10]

Although most poetry, whether written or spoken is RE-cited, its genesis is largely impulsive and intuitive. It is driven by sound and rhythm. In this regard it is improvised. Like other improvised art forms, poetry provides shape, rhythm and tone, without a rigid structure. We see this improvisational character most clearly in rap and other forms of performance poetry.

Poetic leadership is pervasively improvisational, drawing on whatever we have around us, our experiences and resources; weaving our story from snippets and gifts; hearing and working with the rhythmic energy and tone of the workplace; above all being flexible and creative in our approach.

In theatrical and musical improvisation there is said to be no such thing as a mistake; in other words, all mistakes are opportunities. Imperfections in art can create intimacy. From the crazed surface of a raku pot, to the narrative wrinkles of a freshly formed story, we find comfort and space in the vernacular. And we find authenticity and trustworthiness in a leader who shows the flaws of their humanity.

A tolerance of mistakes and imperfections is vital in any creative arena (although it must, of course, must be balanced with safety). If a leader, team or organisation never makes a mistake, it could be argued that they are not stretching themselves enough. A climate of trust and mutual support will make people feel able to make and admit mistakes, and to challenge each other. Innovation requires us to question the status quo and to break the rules.

Vision

Just as a poem should give us a new way to perceive the familiar and open our mind, surprising us with our own new thoughts, so the poetic leader will help people to see in new ways. Leaders must be visionaries; as Shelley said (of poets): *"the hierophants of an unapprehended inspiration; the mirrors of the gigantic shadows which futurity casts upon the present".*

As leaders we have to manage the gap between vision and reality. Without a stretch, no change would happen; too great a leap, and people lose heart.

When an organisation has a genuine shared vision (as opposed to the all-to-familiar 'vision statement'), people excel not because they are told to, but because they want to. A shared picture of the future - of what isn't yet - galvanises people, enrolls support and is further reinforced as it is shared and talked about. The vision becomes clearer, the benefits more imperative, and the approaches to delivery more systemic.

For The Children

The rising hills, the slopes,
of statistics
lie before us.
the steep climb
of everything, going up,
up, as we all
go down.

In the next century
or the one beyond that,
they say,
are valleys, pastures,
we can meet there in peace
if we make it.

To climb these coming crests
one word to you, to
you and your children:

stay together
learn the flowers
go light

Gary Snyder

There is a tension between stability and creativity in everything living, and we experience the movement between stasis and change as rhythm. As Fritjof Capra describes: *"The creativity and adaptability of life expresses itself through the spontaneous emergence of novelty at critical points of instability. Every human organization contains both designed and emergent structures. The challenge is to find the right balance between the creativity of emergence and the stability of design."* [72] As leaders we must manage this ebb and flow between stability and change, vision and reality, action and reflection.

The Rigour of Creativity

Strategists, Platonists, or Benthamites might criticise poetry for a lack of diligence. Yet crafting a poem, like any work of art, is a painstaking process. There is rigour in creativity. As Thomas Fisher writes, *"Creativity involves the intentional, systematic, and rigorous miscombination of what we know in order to generate something new".* [73]

Great poetry requires both backbone and heart; an ability to tackle weighty topics with vim, yet hold intricate ideas with delicacy and precision. It is gutsy and visceral, and at the same time fiercely intelligent.

Poetry as exploration and curiosity

Poets are curious explorers. As Rilke suggested in one of his *Letters to a Young Poet*. "*Have patience with everything that remains unsolved in your heart. Try to love the questions themselves, like locked rooms and like books written in a foreign language.*" [74]

According to Seth Godin, a fundamentalist considers whether a fact is acceptable before they explore it, whereas someone who is innately curious starts with the exploration.[75] Inherently inquisitive people have a desire to understand, and to push the envelope. They are less risk averse than others. The curious are often at the forefront of anything new; they are the early adopters who influence mass opinion; they are leaders.

For innately curious people, as for poets, the process of exploration may be at least as important as any end-point. As film-maker and poet Nic Askew suggests here, the real prize might lie not in definitive answers but in the electricity (or in poetic terms, the *shock*) of the question itself.

The Never Ending Wondering of Why

*A man, wealthy by most of the measures visible to a
first glance, turned his attention to why.
To why he did what he did.
In the hope that it would benefit
his quest for somewhere better.
As he demanded a useful and conclusive answer,
his soul would whisper of a very different possibility.
That such an answer lay hidden in
the electricity of the never-ending wondering of why.*

Nic Askew

Fostering a quiet curiosity is a recurring theme with my coaching clients. Curiosity can keep us learning and creating; it can extend our attention span; curiosity about each other can help to diffuse conflict and tension;. And curiosity about one of our favourite subjects - ourselves - is a vital ingredient in self awareness and emotional intelligence.

19

HEART TO HEART: MAKING CONNECTIONS

Only connect! That was the whole of her sermon.
Only connect the prose and the passion, and both will be exalted,
And human love will be seen at its height.
Live in fragments no longer.
Only connect...

E.M. Forster, *Howards End*

Effective leaders - poetic leaders - honour and nurture connections; in particular people's connection with the things that matter most to them. This is a powerful antidote to the continual erosion of meaning and passion that is common in the superficial churn and aesthetic muteness of many working lives.

Connection & Resonance

In the chapters of this book we have seen how a poem is made not of *either* sound or sense, rhyme or reason, but works as a cohesive whole. As E. M. Forster wrote, "*A poem is true if it hangs together. Information points to something else. A poem points to nothing but itself.*"

So too, great leaders excel by aligning their intellectual, emotional and physical capabilities to maximise performance. In order to truly connect with others, we have to bring all of who we are into relationship. If we are to create true resonance as leaders, we must bring all of our faculties to bear; we must use our head, heart, rhythm, tone, rawness and honesty. We must lead authentically and holistically.

Emotion

W. B. Yeats related how emotional symbolism can "*call down among us certain disembodied powers, whose footsteps over our hearts we call emotions*". [76]

Poetry is the natural habitat of emotional intelligence. Poetry enables us to engage the emotions and helps us *perceive* what we may already know. It works through 'hot' rather than 'cold' cognition, involving the body and all its sensations.

A poem begins as a lump in the throat, a sense of wrong, a homesickness, a lovesickness.

Robert Frost

Our emotions are adaptive devices - finely tuned antennae - that help us negotiate our environment. They grab and direct our attention. Engaging the emotions can help to bring change alive in organisations.

Work presents our greatest opportunity for self-discovery, growth and self-expression, and yet it is often the one place where we are least ourselves. Since work is a powerful force in the shaping of identity, this is a crucial issue. Howard Schechter writes about being our self on the job in his book *Rekindling The Spirit at Work*. Schechter defines spirit not as religion, but as aliveness or enthusiasm (from the Greek *'en theos'* meaning *'filled with God'*).

Organisations tend to be weighted in favour of rational, logical, structural and unemotional modes of operation, rather than more human dimensions. I. A. Richards wrote about poetry as a *humanistic exercise*. He suggested that the best life for a man is one *"in which as much as possible of himself is engaged (as many of his impulses as possible)"* and that such a life *"feels like and is the experience of poetry"*.

A poetic leader may be able to bring more humanism into the workplace. Such emotional intelligence can help us to develop greater awareness of self and others around key drivers (such as values, identity and motives) and to strengthen the follower outcomes of trust, engagement and well-being that lead to sustainable performance.

Relational

I outlined earlier in this book how modern perspectives on leadership, coming from the disciplines of anthropology, sociology and philosophy, suggest that leadership is a *relational* not an individual discipline.

In these perspectives, our leadership "self" is a response to our environment and the other people in it, rather than an expression of an innate persona. The environment in turn is seen not as a fixed reality, but as a co-construction of individuals' minds and their actions.

George Mead for example describes each individual as a *parliament of selves* [77] which arises in the process of social experience and activity. The social conception of self echoes Mikhail Bakhtin's ideas of polyphony and carnival that we saw in Chapter 15.

Effective leaders are visible and open. They don't hide behind hierarchy and bureaucracy, but interact with people across the organisation and inspire them to achievement. They are able to put themselves in others' shoes. The specific relationship between leader and followers is a key part of an organisation's pervading culture.

There is relationship between a poet and their reader, even if that reader is imagined or, indeed, one of the poet's own selves. Poetry needs, and often explicitly seeks, external verification. Only by placing themselves in the role of reader can the poet attempt this verification in advance, to see whether the poem 'works'. A poem must say something new, or in a new way, but it must also somehow fit with the reader's experience of the world so that they have a 'yes' moment. Without this moment, a poem is just words.

Leadership too can only be judged externally; it only matters in action; in relationship. Such relationship is a mirror in which we can see our leadership selves more clearly.

Interpersonal

In the 21st century, enduring business success relies on understanding and responding to the links between the economic, social and environmental subsystems on which we all depend. John Knights, chairman of *LeaderShape*, argues that we therefore need leaders who prioritise the true stakeholders of their organisations (customers, employees, suppliers, the community, the planet, and yes, even the shareholders), rather than personal reward and power. Knights calls such leaders *transpersonal*; a transpersonal leader is one who thinks beyond his or her ego and is *radical, ethical and authentic*. [78]

However hard we, as leaders, strive to be rational and organised - to find the strategies and processes that will guarantee success - this is only a part of why people follow us. The truth is messier and more visceral. We need to put away the presentation pack and truly connect with people. Beyond satisfying basic human needs, people have a deep human yearning to find out what it's all about. Most people are seeking meaning, and connectedness to others and to purpose. They look for leaders who are real; who engage themselves in 'being' leaders as well as 'doing' leadership. They seek in their leaders the right mix of *sense* and *sensibility*.

On Work (extract)

And what is it to work with love?
It is to weave the cloth with threads drawn from your heart,
even as if your beloved were to wear that cloth.
It is to build a house with affection,
even as if your beloved were to dwell in that house.
It is to sow seeds with tenderness and reap the harvest with joy,
even as if your beloved were to eat the fruit.
It is to charge all things you fashion with a breath of your own spirit,
And to know that all the blessed dead
are standing about you and watching.

Kahlil Gibran

Interdependence, Independence & Ego

The most important things at work - the intractable problems and great opportunities - rely on others; they require us to collaborate with other people using high levels of trust, mutual support and synergy. To meet our greatest challenges, we need to embrace our interdependence, and develop the tools and skills we need to make it work effectively. Leaders who happily and visibly rely upon the input of others to deliver their collective vision will foster a strong support base of constituents who willingly follow in their path.

At the same time, the leader needs to be able to operate independently. The credible leader assumes responsibility and accountability; the buck stops with them. People need to see them as reliable and dependable, and as knowing what to do when no-one else does. We therefore need to achieve the tricky balance of achieving trust and connection, whilst supporting the self reliance and independence of the team.

I suggested earlier that poetry and leadership are both best approached in a spirit of humility; with an absence of ego. Art Durkee suggests that one way to practice this in poetry is to move away from first-person narration ("the incessant 'I' of so much contemporary poetry") towards pure description. Without intermediation by poet or narrator, the reader experiences the poetic moment directly and is able to trust in their own feelings, perceptions and judgement. Similarly, if we use less "I" in our leadership, and instead focus on the experiences, feelings and ideas of others, we will empower and engage our followers.

The poet must balance their internal and external drivers for writing: achieving a balance between expressing what is important to them, writing with creative integrity; and appealing to a particular audience, writing what they think others will want to read. So, as leaders, we need to balance the need to develop relationship and connection with a necessary sense of self-sufficiency and integrity.

Ironically, the pressures to succeed as a leader can pull us away from our core values just as we are reinforced by our success. Some people refer to this as CEO-itis. In fact, research suggests that psychotic and anti-social behaviour traits are more prevalent amongst CEOs than in the general population. The aspirant leader might indeed agree with Groucho Marx in this respect: "*I don't want to belong to any club that will accept me as a member.*"

W. H. Auden famously said, "*Put poetry on a pedestal and it ends up on the shelf*". The role of the celebrity leader can be equally isolating - on top of a pedestal is a lonely place. It is also dangerous; worshipped leaders can become defended, invulnerable and arrogant. In healthy organisations, people are empowered to speak their own views, rather than serving as disenfranchised echoes to narcissistic leaders. Like the Emperor with no clothes, leaders need to be told the truth; they need to understand their failings and admit their mistakes; above all they need to connect with others and offer them realistic role models.

Leadership conversations

Modern leadership requires the knotting together of vision, mission and values into meaningful action. It necessitates the continual challenging of the status quo and the frequent reframing of limiting beliefs. To achieve this, we need to use leadership conversations to enthuse and enroll people in the vocation of the business, not simply through strategic leadership decisions and mission statements, but in the quotidian decisions and conversations that engage people's energy.

In an organisation that empowers people, there is good dialogue. The leader helps others to express themselves; they create the overall shape of conversation like curating the exhibits in a museum or the stanzas of a poem.

A poetic leader pays attention, treads lightly, and notices little things; they are full of care and care-ful; they want to see as well as be seen; they are a voice that listens, that asks questions. To listen well we must be genuinely curious about another's point of view; we must hold our own knowledge and authority in abeyance. As Winston Churchill said, *"Courage is what it takes to stand up and speak; courage is also what it takes to sit down and listen."*

In good conversation speech flows; the topic takes over and leads us, rather than us it; the discussion takes on different shapes and forms. Good dialogue turns into a journey of discovery, down a road less travelled, rather than a hike to a fixed destination. Rushing towards a decision might bring some sense of achievement but can crowd out the richness of dialogue.

Genuine dialogue liberates us as leaders from having to know the answers. Instead we need to develop ways of being in conversation that allow those answers to surface; to create conversational spaces. We can create physical spaces and times for dialogue, but above all we must create space IN our conversations. By pausing, deliberating and leaving room for silence, we can nurture an ebb and flow in conversation and in power, that will build wisdom and connection.

Executive Coach and Leadership Embodiment teacher Amanda Ridings describes it thus: *"Making a silence creates roominess and a space for truly listening to self and to others. It slows down a conversation, enabling thinking to emerge and interrupting any tendency to perpetually recycle ... (habitual) ... thoughts."* [79]

Listen: nothing. The sound of silence. The rustle of air in the silence. The music of air touching itself - silently.

Luce Irigaray

Building Trust

A glance at any daily newspaper will confirm that a lack of trust is one of the most crucial issues facing leaders, businesses and public sector organisations today.

How can we build trust? One approach is to open ourselves up - to challenge and suggestions; to compromise; to the possibility of being wrong or of not having all the answers. Being capable of seeing another's point of view - accepting that people on the other side of an issue may be right - is key to connection and empathy. The managerial rhetoric is decisiveness and invulnerability; we need an antidote.

As a grammar of ambiguity, poetry can strengthen our ability to sit with the questions rather than rush to conclusions. This makes it what Clare Morgan calls a *"ground for surrender"*; a place of opening up that can act as a basis for reframing seemingly intractable issues. Reframing and revisioning are essential in opening up the possibility of change of mind; and that possibility, in turn, can act as a catalyst in the trust process.

Common Ground

We can engender trust, and build morale and commitment by involving people in the creation of a shared picture of the future. This is far more effective and sustainable than trying to dictate our own personal vision, no matter how well thought out and heartfelt. Enthusiasm created in this way is contagious, and the vision gains clarity and traction through ongoing dialogue and re-telling.

Co-creation of vision is especially vital in times of organisational change, when people most fear a loss of control or freedom. Often their resistance is not to change itself, but to the way in which it is imposed.

Collaborative leaders seek out that which unifies, and direct their energy to that which brings and holds people together, rather than to anatomising their differences; yet they need to do this without imposing a impersonal world view.

Poets, too, search for universally understandable symbols that are nevertheless made personal. As Keith Holyoak [2] argues, *"Poetry reflects the tension between what is personal and what is collective, individuality and the shared human core..."* adding *"if symbols don't move the poet, the result is a dry intellectual exercise. If they don't move the listener or reader, the poem has surely failed."*

Just as poet and audience must share symbols if they are to share a poem, leader and followers need to find a common language that each can use in their own way.

Such a language can be brought to life through specific detail rather than the vague and impersonal language we often hear in organisations. Stephen Denning suggests that in putting forward their ideas in abstract generalities, individuals are *"unwittingly going into control modes of interaction in order to fend off inklings of their mounting internal self doubt"*, and that *"civilization is resting on a footing of unspoken fear"*. [43] Being specific, being truly seen and heard, perhaps even naming our fears, can deepen our work conversations and connections.

Poetry works by connecting the general with the personal or individual. By writing very specifically, often at an emotional level, of one experience, a good poet can connect to the reader's own specific experience. I like to think of this as finding the *highest common denominator*.

Of course, the poet does not have to be writing autobiographically about an event that has actually happened to them. Rather, they write with an intense understanding of a specific scenario. This doesn't make their words any less true. Like acting, poetry is telling the truth under (often) imaginary circumstances. Even when the event described has actually happened to the poet, the reader's mental picture of it will inevitably be a *different* truth.

Courage

The word courage comes from the Middle English word *corage*, meaning of the heart (cor being equivalent to cuer - heart - in Old French).

Aristotle called courage the first virtue, because it makes all the other virtues possible. Courage informs and strengthens all leadership virtues. In *Leading from Within*, Sam Intrator and Megan Scribner have curated a collection of poems chosen by a wide range of leaders, under the banner of poetry that *'sustains the courage to lead'*. They argue that leadership requires heart, courage, and wisdom, and that these qualities can be inspired and informed by poetry.

It takes courage *not* a lack of fear to lead. Courageous leaders have fear, but they step up and speak out anyway; they take risks; they put themselves onto the stage. And they do it every day:

from *The Abnormal Is Not Courage*

...Not the Prodigal Son, nor Faustus. But Penelope.
The thing steady and clear. Then the crescendo.
The real form. The culmination. And the exceeding.
Not the surprise. The amazed understanding. The marriage,
Not the month's rapture. Not the exception. The beauty
That is of many days. Steady and clear.

Jack Gilbert

The ability to speak difficult truths is one aspect of the courage required of leaders. This is never easy, but it becomes ever more vital, as we take on more senior roles, that we are not swayed by convention or pressure from others. We must continue to set the tone. On the lower slopes of leadership we may have learned how hard it can be to speak the truth (especially to more senior colleagues); in turn we can use this experience to support others on their leadership journey, inviting feedback and challenge from them. We need to show how good leaders are willing to listen to challenging feedback, and to truths.

We have explored courageous aspects of poetic leadership throughout this book, including:

- the courage to take the initiative - to make a mark on a blank sheet
- the courage to let go of the familiar - to be open to the unknown
- the courage to sit with silence and space
- the courage to speak up - to raise difficult issues, give tough feedback and voice unpopular views
- the courage to be humble and undefended
- the courage to be real - to live by our values authentically
- The courage to feel, including to the courage to love, deeply

Having virtue is not enough. It must show up in our actions, decisions and behaviour. As C.S. Lewis observed in *The Screwtape Letters*, "*Courage is not simply one of the virtues, but the form of every virtue at the testing point, which means, at the point of highest reality.*" [80]

Joining The Dots

The point of highest reality for poetic leadership is also at the testing point, in our thoughts and deeds as leaders, whether in private or in public.

If the idea of being a more poetic leader appeals to you, then I invite you to identify and combine those aspects that speak most clearly to you.

If you can connect the premises in this book to your own experience and practice of leadership, then I hope they will provide you not only with some different approaches, but with comfort, clarity and courage.

I also hope that you enjoy the exploration. I'd love to hear about your experiences along the way.

Happy adventuring

Sam

sam@differentdevelopment.com

Courage

Courage is the price that
Life exacts for granting peace.

The soul that knows it not
Knows no release from little things:
Knows not the livid loneliness of fear,
Nor mountain heights where bitter joy can hear the sound of wings.

Nor can life grant us boon of living, compensate
For dull gray ugliness and pregnant hate
Unless we dare
The soul's dominion.
Each time we make a choice, we pay
With courage to behold the resistless day,
And count it fair.

Amelia Earhart

BIBLIOGRAPHY

Aristotle. *Poetics*

Attali, J. *Noise: The Political Economy of Music.* University of Minnesota Press, 1977.

Avolio, B.J., & Gardner, W.L. *Authentic leadership development: Getting to the root of positive forms of leadership.* The Leadership Quarterly, 16 (2005), 315-338.

Ayot, W. *Email for the Soul.* PS Avalon, 2012

Bettelheim, B. *The Uses of Enchantment: The Meaning and Importance of Fairy Tales.* Penguin, 1991.

Black, M. *Models and Metaphors.* Cornell University Press, 1962.

Carroll, L. Through The Looking Glass. 1871.

Clutterbuck, D. and Megginson, D. *Mentoring Executives and Directors.* Butterworth Heinemann, 1999.

Coleridge, S. T. *Biographia literaria,* 1817

De Pree, M. *Leadership is an Art.* Doubleday, 1989.

Denning, S. *The Springboard: How Storytelling Ignites Action in Knowledge-Era Organizations.* Butterworth Heinemann, 2000.

Drucker, P. *The Practice of Management.* Heinemann, 1955.

Doyle, M. E. and Smith, M. K. *Classical models of managerial leadership: trait, behavioural, contingency and transformational theory.* The encyclopedia of informal education, 2001

Durkee, A. *Notes towards an egoless poetry.* DragonCave. (artdurkee.blogspot.co.uk), 2006

Fry, S. *The Ode Less Travelled: Unlocking The Poet Within.* Arrow, 2007.

George, W. G. *Authentic leadership: rediscovering the secrets to creating lasting value.* Jossey-Bass, 2004

Godin, S. *Tribes: We need you to lead us.* Piatkus, 2008.

Goens, G. *Leadership and Poetry*. Retrieved 24 August 2014 from http://033b364.netsolhost.com/rt_juxta_wp-rocketlauncher/wp-content/uploads/2011/06/Leadership_and_Poetry-George_A_Goens.pdf

Grint, K. *The Arts of Leadership*. Oxford University Press, 2000.

Geary, J. *I Is an Other: The Secret Life of Metaphor and How It Shapes the Way We See the World*. Harper, 2011

Hersey, P. and Blanchard, K. H. *Management of Organizational Behavior: Utilizing Human Resources*. Prentice Hall, 1972

Housman, A E. *The Name and Nature of Poetry*. Lecture at Cambridge University, 1933

Intrator, S. M. and Scribner, M. *Leading from Within: Poetry That Sustains the Courage to Lead*. Jossey-Bass, 2007

James, W. *The Meaning of Truth*. Project Gutenburg, 1909

Kets de Vries, M. and Balazs, K. *The Shadow Side of Leadership* in Bryman, A. et al (eds) *The SAGE Handbook of Leadership*. SAGE Publications Ltd., 2011

Kline, N. *Time To Think - Listening To Ignite The Human Mind*. Cassell Illustrated, 1999

Krieger, M. *The New Apologists for Poetry*. Minnesota University Press, 1956

Ladkin, D. *Leading beautifully: How mastery, congruence and purpose create the aesthetic of embodied leadership practice*. The Leadership Quarterly 19 (2008) 31–41.

Lakoff, G. & Johnson, M. *Metaphors We Live By*. University of Chicago Press, April 2003

Lewis, T., Amini, F. and Lannon, R. *A General Theory of Love*. Vintage Books, 2001

Morgan, C. *What Poetry Brings to Business*. The University of Michigan Press, 2010

Murdock, M. *The Heroine's Journey*. Shambhala Publications Inc, 1990

Northouse, P. *Leadership: Theory and Practice*. Sage, 2012

Okri, B. A Way of Being Free. Phoenix Press. 1997.

Palmer, P. *Let your life speak.* John Wiley & Sons, 1999

Palmer, W. *The Intuitive Body.* Blue Snake Books, 2008

Perera, S. B. *Descent to the Goddess.* Inner City Books, 1981

Prose, F. *Reading Like a Writer: A Guide for People Who Love Books and for Those Who Want to Write Them.* Union Books, 2012

Richards, I. A. *Science and Poetry.* Haskell House, 1926

Schechter, H. *Rekindling The Spirit at Work.* Barrytown/Station Hill Press, Inc., 2010

Senge, P. *The Fifth Discipline: The Art & Practice of the Learning Organization.* Doubleday Business, 1990

Steiner, R. *The human being's experience of tone.* In *Art in the light of mystery wisdom.* Rudolf Steiner Press, 1970

Tavris, C., and Aronson, E. *Mistakes Were Made (But Not by Me): Why We Justify Foolish Beliefs, Bad Decisions, and Hurtful Acts.* Mariner Books, 2008

Walker, S P. *The undefended leader.* Piquant Editions, 2010

Wall, T. and Knights, J. *Leadership Assessment for Talent Development.* Kogan Page, 2013

Warner, M. *From The Beast To The Blonde: On Fairy Tales and Their Tellers.* Vintage, 1995

Weick, K. E. *Sensemaking in Organizations.* (Foundations for Organizational Science), SAGE, 1995

Whyte, D. *The Heart Aroused: Poetry and the Preservation of the Soul in Corporate America.* Doubleday, 1994

Wittgenstein, L. *Philosophical Investigations, 1953.* Wiley-Blackwell,2009

Wright, P. *Managerial Leadership.* Routledge, 1996

Zander, R. S. and Zander, B. *The Art of Possibility.* Harvard Business School Press, 2000

ACKNOWLEDGEMENTS

I am deeply grateful to the many people who have encouraged me in the creation of this book, and to those who have generously given time, words or financial backing to make it what it is, including everyone who backed the Kickstarter project to support the first print run. I am also indebted to the poetic leaders, in many guises, that I have met and worked with.

Very special thanks are due to:

Amanda Ridings

Michaela Ridgway

Kathryn Ghent

Nick Carver

PERMISSIONS

POEMS

Not there, not yet by Art Durkee (www.arthurdurkee.net) by permission of the author

Juggling in Church, Don Barnard by permission of the author

The Riddle of Here by Nic Askew (nicaskew.com) by permission of the author

Hairless by Jo Shapcott from *Of Mutability*, Faber and Faber, 2011. By permission of the publisher.

In The Margins by Rachael Clyne by permission of the author

Betweenland X by Philip Gross in *The Water Table*, Bloodaxe, 2009 by permission of the author

Wedding by Alice Oswald in *The Thing in the Gap-Stone Stile*, Faber & Faber Ltd., 2007 by permission of the author

Ablutions by Michaela Ridgway. By permission of the author.

Ghazal of the Better-Unbegun by Heather McHugh from *The Father of the Predicaments*, Wesleyan University Press, 1999. © 2001 Heather McHugh. Reprinted by permission of the Wesleyan Press.

Personal Helicon for Michael Longley by Seamus Heaney, from *Death of a Naturalist*, Faber & Faber, 2006. By permission of the publisher.

Command by Rachel Barenblat from *70 Faces*, Phoenicia Publishing, 2011. By permission of the author and Phoenicia Publishing.

The Makers by Howard Nemerov from *Sentences,* University of Chicago Press, 1981 by permission of Alexander Nemerov.

Why I seldom talk to strange women at parties. Mark Woodward, © MW 3/4/2013. By permission of the author.

The Waste Land by T.S Eliot, Faber & Faber, 1922. By permission of the publisher.

Wind by Ted Hughes from *The Hawk in the Rain*. Faber & Faber, 1957. By permission of the publisher.

Thirty spokes meet at a nave, from the *Tao Te Ching* by Lao Tzu. Translation © Peter A. Merel. www.chinapage.com/gnl.html

Asphodel, That Greeny Flower by William Carlos Williams, From *Collected*

Extract from *One Art* by Elizabeth Bishop from *Complete Poems,* Chatto and Windus, 2004. Reprinted with the permission of Randomhouse

Climbing Above Rongbuk Monastery by Keith Holyoak from *Foreigner: New English Poems in Chinese Old Style. Dos Madres Press: Loveland, Ohio, 2012. By permission of the author.*

Sufi Wisdom by Rumi from *Rumi Wisdom – Daily Teachings from the Great Sufi Master* by Timothy Freke, Sterling, 2000

Knowledge by Philip Memmer from *Threat of Pleasure,* Word Press, 2008. By permission of the author

The Turn by Jalal al-Din Rumi in *The Essential Rumi*, Coleman Barks (tr) Harper SanFrancisco; 7th edition, 2004

For The Children - Gary Snyder from Turtle Island, 1974 © 1974 by Gary Snyder. Reprinted by permission of New Directions Publishing Corp.

The Never Ending Wondering of Why by Nic Askew (nicaskew.com) by permission of the author

The Abnormal Is Not Courage by Jack Gilbert, © Jack Gilbert.

QUOTES

Permission to use quotations as cited in the references has been very kindly given by the following:

Keith Holyoak, David Morley, George Szirtes, Mary Catherine Bateson, John Felstiner, Colwyn Trevarthen, Jane Holland, Rachel Blau DuPlessis, The Minghella family, Trish Greenhalgh, Lisa Rossetti, Philip Davis, Daniel Pink, Amantha Imber, John Knights, Amanda Ridings, Nic Askew, Karl Weick, Nancy Kline, Art Durkee

The following permissions are also gratefully acknowledged:

"Author's Introduction (The Wedge)" By William Carlos Williams, from Selected Essays of William Carlos Williams, ©1954 by William Carlos Williams. Reprinted by permission of New Directions Publishing Corp.

DISCLAIMER

This book is a low budget, self published endeavor. Whilst I believe its blend of concepts to be unique, my thinking draws from a rich seam of existing material. I have sought permission to use the poems and any substantial quotes, and have cited other material under fair use guidelines. However, practice around copyright and permissions is notoriously complex. If I have inadvertently quoted your words without permission, please let me know and I will try to put it right.

REFERENCES

1. Zander, R. S. and Zander, B. *The Art of Possibility*. Harvard Business School Press, 2000

2. Holyoak, K. *What should a poem be like?* In *Rhyme and Reason - Modern Formal Poetry*. McAlister, N. H. (ed.). McAlister, 2006

3. Pogacnik, Miha. quoted in Darso, L. *Artful Creation: Learning-tales of Arts-in-business*. Samfundslitteratur, (2004)

4. Barr, J. in the introduction to Morgan, C. *What Poetry Brings to Business*. The University of Michigan Press, 2010

5. Arnold, M. *The Study of Poetry*. Essays: English and American, The Harvard Classics, 1994

6. Heidegger, M. *On the Origin of the Work of Art*, ed. Krell, D. F. Harper Collins, 2008.

7. Holzer, B N. *A Walk Between Heaven & Earth*. Bell Tower, 1994.

8. Avolio, B. J., & Gardner, W. L., *Authentic leadership development: Getting to the root of positive forms of leadership*. The Leadership Quarterly, 16, (2005), 315-338

9. Morley, D. www2.warwick.ac.uk/fac/cross_fac/prizeforwriting/about/

10. Bateson, M. C. *Composing a Life*. Atlantic Monthly Press, 1989.

11. Gadamer, H-G., *The Relevance of the Beautiful and Other Essays*, Cambridge University Press, 1986

12. Paterson, D. Interview with M. Fazzini. www.donpaterson.com, 2003

13. Shklovsky, V. *Form and Material in Art*, in *Dissonant Voices in Soviet Literature*. Eds. Blake, P. and Hayward, M. Pantheon Books, 2012..

14. Read, H. *English Prose Style*, Random House, 1981

15. Felstiner, J. *Paul Celan: Poet, Survivor, Jew*. Yale University Press, 2001

16. Szirtes, G. *The Sweetest Sound of All*. The Guardian, 21 November, 2005.

17. Roth, G. *Maps to Ecstasy: The Healing Power of Movement*. New World Library, 2003.

18. Stafford, W. E. *You Must Revise Your Life*. University of Michigan Press, 1987

19. Grossman, D. Interview with T. Sutcliffe on Front Row, BBC Radio 4, 21 February, 2014. www.bbc.co.uk/programmes/p01svysq

20. Frost, R. Interview with S Bowen in *A Poet on the Campus of the University of Michigan*, Detroit News, Nov. 27, 1921

21. Trevarthen, C. *Musicality and the Intrinsic Motive Pulse: Evidence from human psychobiology and infant communication*. In *Rhythms, musical narrative, and the origins of human communication*. Musicae Scientiae, Fall 1999-2000 vol. 3 no. 1 suppl 155-215.

22. Wason, P. C. Journal of the American Medical Association, cited in Rhythm & Work, Time Magazine, Monday, Apr. 25, 1955. www.time.com/time/magazine/article/0,9171,861407,00.html

23. Rogers, R. A. *Rhythm and the performance of organisation*. Text and performance quarterly 14 (1994): 222-237

24. Olson, S. *Projective Verse* from *Collected Prose*, eds. Allen, D. and Friedlander, B., University of California Press, 1950

25. Guaïtella, I. *Rhythm in speech: What rhythmic organizations reveal about cognitive processes in spontaneous speech production versus reading aloud*. Journal of Pragmatics. Volume 31, Issue 4 (1999): 509-523

26. Williams, W. C. *Introduction to The Wedge*, in *Selected Essays of William Carlos Williams*. New Directions, 1969.

27. Wheatley, M. J. *Leadership and the New Science: Discovering Order in a Chaotic World*. Berrett-Koehler Publishers, Inc., 2006

28. Denhardt, B. and Denhardt, J. *The Dance of Leadership*, M.E. Sharpe, 2006

29. Yeats, W. B. *The Symbolism of Poetry* in *Ideas of Good and Evil*. A H Bullen, 1903

30. Mumford, L. *The Myth of the Machine*. Secker & Warburg, 1967

31. Morley, D. *On Form*. http://www2.warwick.ac.uk/fac/arts/english/currentstudents/undergraduate/modules/fulllist/second/en238/workshop_on_form/ Retrieved 14/9/14

32. Miller, J. H. On *W C Williams' Asphodel, That Greeny Flower,* in *Poets of Reality: Six Twentieth-Century Writers.* Harvard University, 1965

33. Holland, J. *Notes towards authenticity.* Raw Light, May 12, 2014. rawlightblog.blogspot.co.uk/2014/05/notes-towards-authenticity.html

34. Simons, T. L. *Behavioral integrity as a critical ingredient for transformational leadership,* Journal of Organizational Change Management, Vol. 12 (1999) Iss. 2: 89 - 104

35. Peck, E. and Dickinson, H. *Performing Leadership.* Palgrave Macmillan; 2009

36. Diemand-Yauman, C., et al. *Fortune favors the Bold (and the italicized): Effects of disfluency on educational outcomes.* Cognition (2010), doi: 10.1016/j.cognition.2010.09.012

37. DuPlessis, R. B. *Blue Studios: Poetry and Its Cultural Work.* University Alabama Press, 2006. © Rachel Blau DuPlessis. All rights reserved

38. Minghella, A. *Minghella on Minghella.* Faber & Faber, 2005

39. Pinkola Estes, C. *Women Who Run With The Wolves: Contacting the Power of the Wild Woman.* Rider, 2008

40. Campbell, J. *The Hero with a Thousand Faces.* Novato, California: New World Library, 2008, p. 23.

41. Greenhalgh, P. et al. *Narrative methods in quality improvement research.* Qual. Saf. Health Care; 14 (2005); 443-449

42. Okri, B. *No. 1* in *Aphorisms and Fragments from The Joys of Storytelling* in *A Way of Being Free. (idem).*

43. Denning, S. *The Springboard: How Storytelling Ignites Action in Knowledge-Era Organizations.* Butterworth Heinemann, 2000

44. Rossetti, L. *Storytelling for Talent Development* in Wall, T and Knights, J. (eds.) *Leadership Assessment for Talent Development.* Kogan Page, 2013.

45. Gabriel, Y. *The Unmanaged Organization: Stories, Fantasies and Subjectivity.* Organization Studies. Vol. 16 (1995) No. 3: 477-501

46. Bakhtin, M. M. *Problems of Dostoevsky's Poetics.* University of Minnesota Press, 1984

47. Frost, R. *The Figure A Poem Makes.* from *Collected Poems of Robert Frost.* Holt, Rinehart, and Winston, 1939.

48. Santayana, G. *The Elements and Function of Poetry*, Chapter 10 in *Interpretations of Poetry and Religion.* Harper & Brothers, 1957

49. Weick, K. E. *The Social Psychology of Organizing.* Random House, 1979

50. Lessing, G. E. *Laocoon. An essay upon the limits of painting and poetry.* Roberts Brothers, 1887

51. Davis, P. et al. *The Shakespeared Brain.* The Reader. No. 23 (2011): 39-43

52. March, J. G., *Poetry and the Rhetoric of Management: Easter 1916,* Journal of Management Inquiry. Vol. 15 (2006). No. 1: 70-72

53. Ammons, A R. *Paper to the international poetry forum,* Pittsburgh, 1967

54. Gibbs, R. *Poetics of Mind*, Cambridge University Press, 1994

55. Spender, S. *The Imagination in the Modern World*, U.S. Govt. Printing Office, Washington, D.C., 1962

56. Saul, J. R. Voltaire's Bastards: The Dictatorship of Reason in the West. Penguin Putnam Inc., 1994

57. Bruner, J. *On Knowing: Essays for the Left Hand*, Loeb Classical Library, 1962

58. Taylor, J. B. *My Stroke of Insight.* Hodder Paperbacks, 2009.

59. Gladwin, T., *East is a Big Bird: Navigation and Logic on Puluwat Atoll*, Harvard University Press, 1995

60. Shklovsky, V. *Art as Technique.* In Lee & Reiss, *Russian Formalist Criticism.* University of Nebraska Press, 2012

61. Damasion, A. *Descartes' Error: Emotion, Reason and the Human Brain.* Vintage, 2006

62. Nussbaum, M. *Love's Knowledge.* Oxford University Press, 1990

63. Bohm, D. *On dialogue.* Routledge, 1996

64. Orr, J. E. and Sack, K. *Building the Leadership Skills that Matter* Korn/Ferry International, ,2009

65. Tsur, R. *'Kubla Khan' - Poetic Structure, Hypnotic Quality, and Cognitive*

Style: A Study in Mental, Vocal, and Critical Performance. John Benjamins Publishing, 2006

66. Keats, J. In a letter to his brother George, 1817

67. IBM, *Capitalizing on Complexity. Insights from the 2010 IBM Global CEO Study.* http://www-935.ibm.com/services/us/ceo/ceostudy2010/index.html, 2010

68. Pink, D. H. *A Whole New Mind: Why Right-brainers Will Rule the Future.* Marshall Cavendish, 2008

69. Imber, A. Predicting the unpredictable. innovationtools.com www.inventium.com.au

70. Bohr, N. quoted by Heisenberg, W. (tr. Pomerans, A. J.) in *Physics and Beyond: Encounters and Conversations,* HarperCollins Publishers Ltd., 1971

71. Spender, S. *Chaos and Control in Poetry.* U.S. Govt. Printing Office; Washington, 1966

72. Capra, F. *Life and Leadership: A Systems Approach.* www.fritjofcapra.net

73. Fisher, T. *The Rigor of Creativity.* TED Weekends: Imagination Innovation. Huffington Post. December 14, 2012

74. Rilke, R. M. *Letters to a Young Poet,* Norton, 1934

75. Godin, S. *On Curiosity.* Video by N Askew, soulbiographies.com, 2007

76. Yeats, W. B. *Ideas of good and evil.* A. H. Bullen, 1903

77. Mead, G. H. *Mind, Self, and Society,* ed. Morris C. W. University of Chicago, 1934

78. Knights, J. *The Invisible Elephant & The Pyramid Treasure,* Tomorrow's Company, 2012

79. Ridings, A. *Pause for Breath: Bringing the practices of mindfulness and dialogue to leadership conversations.* Live It, 2011

80. Lewis, C. S. *The Screwtape Letters,* XXIX © copyright CS Lewis Pte Ltd., Geoffrey Bles: the Centenary Press, 1942